"Grace is a contagious force we all crave and Maria contains so much grace it floods you from just a short time with her. May these pages overwhelm you with God's love, and hope that Maria knows so well."

Jennie Allen, founder of IF: Gathering
and author of *Nothing to Prove*

"I've had the chance to visit many places over the years. Finding the purpose behind the places I go always intrigues me. I've been to Maria's home and I know its purpose. It's simply a place where love lives. You're going to enjoy reading in these pages about how we can each make the places where we live places where love lives too."

Jeremy Cowart, photographer
and founder of the Purpose Hotel

"Maria and her words are a gift to everyone searching for love, meaning, and a place to belong. My life is brighter and my heart is bigger because of what I experienced on these pages. I cried. I smiled. I felt loved. It's an absolutely incredible book!"

Mike Foster, author of *People of the Second Chance: A Guide To Bringing Life-Saving Love to the World*

"What a gift to read *Love Lives Here* and find within it a friend who is as authentic and inviting as Maria Goff. Through her earnest telling of the stories of her life, she provides greater meaning to all our lives. We were thrilled to read this book."

Donald Miller, best-selling author of
Blue Like Jazz and *Scary Close*, and **Betsy Miller**

"In a moment in my life when I was desperately looking for direction, God used my friendship with Maria to rekindle in me a long-held vision for hospitality that I'd allowed to be obscured by far less important things. This beautiful book will do that same sacred work for so many people. Maria is an example to me—the kind of mother I aspire to be, the kind of gatherer of people I aspire to be. I'm so very thankful for this lovely book, and the heart and wisdom written on every page."

Shauna Niequist, *New York Times* best-selling author of *Present Over Perfect* and *Savor*

"Through every page, I loved discovering the powerful, mighty woman whose gentle voice and warm heart belie her strength. Maria opens the door of her heart to reveal life is found in rubble, in broken dreams, in oozing hot lava, and—most importantly—love is found in the places we least expect it. With every chapter I felt welcomed into her home, invited to pull up a chair and sit and listen to how to love, live, and act toward others. Not only did I walk away wanting a friend like Maria, I wanted to grow up and BE Maria Goff."

Bianca Juarez Olthoff, best-selling author of *Play with Fire*

"This book is the hug you didn't know you've always needed. Maria's words of hope, purpose, and vulnerability ring true in the deepest parts of my soul, inspiring me to live and love better."

Ryan O'Neal, Sleeping at Last

"Maria has cultivated a beautiful heart and home where the Lord dwells richly. *Love Lives Here* shows us how we can experience amazing joy from the inside out. This book will change you and your family."

Lysa TerKeurst, *New York Times* best-selling author and president of Proverbs 31 Ministries

"Maria Goff is the wise, gracious, and witty mentor you always wanted. With hospitality and vulnerability, she invites you to sit in the coziest chair of her home, warm cup in hand, as she tells you her stories. And in the telling, you hear anew your own stories and God's stories, too."

Katherine and Jay Wolf, coauthors of *Hope Heals: A True Story of Overwhelming Loss and an Overcoming Love* and co-founders of Hope Heals

"*Love Lives Here* is every bit as warm and kind as you'd expect from an author known to most of the world as Sweet Maria. But its warmth does not diminish the truth it poignantly and consistently delivers. Reading like a memoir and a lesson book, this collection of vignettes does not stop at being a window into Sweet Maria Goff's life, but rather, it's an invitation to step right into her life. If you love the feeling of gaining a new best friend, read this book. If you've ever wondered how a life some may consider quiet can incrementally impact the world, read this book."

Shelley Giglio, chief strategist, sixstepsrecords, and co-founder of Passion Conferences/Passion City Church

LOVE

FINDING WHAT YOU NEED IN A WORLD

LIVES

TELLING YOU WHAT YOU WANT

HERE

MARIA GOFF

B&H

PUBLISHING GROUP

NASHVILLE, TENNESSEE

978-1-4336-4891-5

Published by B&H Publishing Group
Nashville, Tennessee

Dewey Decimal Classification: 306.85
Subject Heading: CHRISTIAN LIFE \ FAMILY LIFE \
DOMESTIC RELATIONS

Author is respresented by Alive Literary Agency,
7680 Goddard Street, Suite 200, Colorado Springs, CO 80920,
www.aliveliterary.com.

1 2 3 4 5 6 7 • 21 20 19 18 17

For my kids' kids' kids, and all of the generations to come.

Contents

Foreword

by Bob Goff

None of us really fall in love. We just stop making everything about ourselves, and love floods into the space selfishness leaves behind when it leaves the room. That's what happened to me when I met Maria thirty-two years ago.

I wasn't looking for a wife at the time. That is, until I met Maria—then I was looking for a wife. Here was my problem: She wasn't looking for me. When you find the right person, something changes inside of you. Food doesn't taste the same, movies aren't as entertaining as they used to be, and hanging out with your friends doesn't sound as fun anymore. All you want to do is be together with the person you've given your heart away to. I think God wired us from the factory for this kind of love and connection. Love without connection doesn't have much shelf life. Neither does connection without love.

After trying to get Maria to like me back for quite a while, I took a knee and got out a partial, heart-in-the-throat marriage proposal to her. It was only partial, because right after I got out the words "Maria, will you . . . ?" I got all choked up and couldn't finish the sentence. You see, I'm emotionally incontinent—which is a real problem if you're a trial lawyer.

Maria leaned down and gently held my face in her hands and said, "Marry me?" I nodded yes and she nodded yes, too.

None of us complete each other, but we can add a few words to the lives of the people around us to help them understand God's bigger plan for all of us. This is what Maria has done in this book. She's offered a few words to help us understand what she has been learning from Jesus while she's been loving her family and the people around her.

I'm a lawyer. I memorize things for a living. The things I'm still trying to memorize about love and faith and people, Maria just does naturally. Don't get me wrong. She's not perfect by any means. If you give her a box of See's candy, she'll take one out, bite the bottom off and if she doesn't like it, she'll put the part of the candy she didn't eat back in the box. What kind of a person does that and doesn't even feel bad about it? That's just wrong.

A man named Paul wrote letters to his friends, which make up a great deal of the Bible. In one of those letters he said that God would finish what He started in us. Just like Maria finished my halting proposal, I'm banking on the notion that God isn't finished with any of us yet. I bet heaven can't wait to see what sentences He'll complete through each of us. Still, we need to start it, so He can complete it. This book is about starting where love lives— in your home, in your neighborhood, and in your life.

It's been more than thirty years since Maria and I said "I do," and she's still completing my sentences. I'm glad she does, too, because she makes mine better when she does. Authentic love does this for each of us. It whispers the words we're missing and is gracious enough to let us think we came up with them ourselves. The words in this book aren't just good. Good words are pretty easy to find. Almost anyone can come up with a few of them. These words are true, which is a little less common. They aren't just words about hopes either; they're about what happens when you actually let love invade your heart, your family, and your home. A lot of people want a great life; what I've watched Maria do is live a great life.

Maria isn't like me. In many ways you couldn't find two more different people. I'm outgoing and loud and wave my arms in the air a lot. Being around people is oxygen to me. The more, the better. In contrast, Maria is wise and brilliant and kind and shy. She thinks having me in the room is a lot of people. Seeing Maria at an event is like spotting a unicorn. Everyone likes talking to Maria because she is humble and loving and lives entirely without pretense or disguise. She doesn't need the attention or validation my own insecurity demands. She's able to do this for one reason. She knows who she is and finds her security in Jesus rather than finding it in other people's approval.

It's not easy living with a guy who lives like Red Bull sponsors him. John Wesley wrote in his diary at age eighty-three, "Laziness is slowly setting in; I am finding it increasingly difficult to get out of bed before five in the morning." I can relate. When espresso needs to wake up, it drinks me. Most of the time, I feel like the dog in the movie *Up* getting distracted by a squirrel. I get up with the chickens every day full of ideas and ready to start something new. Maria has been wise enough to pick things that last long enough for her to continue to work on each day. She takes things like her family and her faith and her friends so seriously, she's not head-faked by the transient distractions that get me off message. Unfortunately, all of this energy has been driving the people I love the most nuts. Nevertheless,

Maria always knows the right things to say to me at just the right times. She doesn't need to fight for my attention; people who are devoted to the things Jesus talked about get it without needing to ask.

Maria says I'm addicted to happiness. She knows all about personality profiles and reminds me often of which one fits me. Until I met her, I thought an Enneagram was a breakfast cereal. When I say something that's just a little too happy for the circumstances or get distracted by my own enthusiasm, she'll say, "A *seven* always does that." Perhaps. Still, she helps me get ready in the morning so I don't run out the front door with one pant leg tucked into my sock. Apparently, *sevens* do that too. We're not trying to figure each other out; we're trying to find each other out. Figuring each other out sounds like a project; finding each other out sounds like an adventure together.

We all sort through piles of other people's words every day, sometimes without even knowing we're doing it. The best words don't really find us; we find them. Eventually, we pick a couple for ourselves and start using them to describe what matters most to us. Once we've picked all of the words we have time to pick, we call it our life. I've been trying to pick better words. Kinder and more generous words. Most of the best words I've found about love and faith and family I've learned from Maria.

There are plenty of things I don't know about. I don't know what makes us yawn or why some people are right-handed and others left, or why you can't fold a piece of paper more than seven times, but this I'm certain of: We'll be known for our opinions, but we'll be remembered for our love. Maria has spent her whole life loving people, and it's what she'll be remembered for. She's helped our family pick more accurate words and less distracting ones, more encouraging words and less critical ones, more authentic words and less phony ones. She didn't do this by telling us what to say, but by showing us how to live.

I'll tell you one last thing about Maria. One time when I was stuck while I was working on a writing project, she sent me this text message: "Every word in the universe is hoping you'll pick them." Kind words from the people we love have the power to help us all understand who we are and what we want our lives to mean. Of all of the words ever spoken, the words in this book are the ones Maria picked for us. They're good, they're true, and they will lead you home. Let me introduce to you the most humble and impressive woman I've ever met in my life, my wife, Sweet Maria Goff.

Introduction

When I was young, there was a small pond near our home. I would drop small sticks in the water and watch them lay suspended on the surface. The ripples would go outward as I would lean over, blow a puff of wind, and then watch the mirror-like surface go dark with small ripples and carry my stick to the other side. This wasn't any old piece of wood; it was a courageous vessel—able to stand up against the tallest seas the pond could throw at it. In my young mind, I was the wind, I made the waves, and I was the boat.

Over the years, more wind blew in my life, just like it might have done in yours, and I discovered that I was neither the wind nor the waves nor the boat. I was just the confused kid on the edge of the pond looking at my reflection and trying to understand who it was that I was looking at.

I didn't write this book because I think we need more information, more steps, or more instructions on how to lead a meaningful life. Instead, I think we all can benefit from times of honest reflection. It's not often that we have the chance to lean over our own lives and try to make sense of them.

The pages in this book are the vignettes of my life I came across when I began leaning over mine and took a hard look at who God had made me to be. To do this, I couldn't just look on the surface, I had to go deeper. Not surprisingly, I've learned a couple things while doing this. I've been reminded that we are not the things we've done nor the things which have been done to us. We're not the successes we've had or the painful mistakes we've made. Instead, each of us is a reflection of Jesus amongst all of these things that have occurred in our lives. My hope is that you find some portion of your unique and God-given reflection in these pages just as I did while writing them.

The stories in this book are about the people I love the most and what I've learned from them. It's about blowing it and having a patient God remind me that it's His pond we're playing in, not ours. It's about finding the courage to launch more sticks when the ones I valued the most were lost at sea. I wrote this book because I decided that getting to the other side of the pond was worth the effort involved in the crossing and that the way across lies beneath the surface.

We all have a couple versions of ourselves, perhaps more. One is the kid with the stick, a chest full of wind, and a childlike faith. This is the version of ourselves that some of us have cheerfully found and others have reluctantly lost. Paul said in one of his letters to a friend named James that sometimes life is like looking in a mirror and then forgetting our appearance. I think I know what he meant. I remember as a young person seeing myself in the reflection on the surface of the water. I saw someone who was young, cheerful, full of energy and hope and courage. Soon, the busyness of life happened and I forgot what that person looked like. To be honest, I welcomed this because I'm not proud of what many of my younger years held.

Sometimes we try to forget our past. We mask it, or medicate it, or try to ignore it completely, but we can only outrun it for a while. Eventually, we need to return to the pond, see our reflections again, and understand who we are now, by remembering where we've been. It takes some heavy lifting to do this, and I've needed to do the majority of it from my knees. But understanding who God wants me to become has been worth the work, because it made me look beneath the surface of my life. I hope there will be something in this book that will help you look beneath yours, too.

Most of us don't even remember when we walked away from our pond. We don't know why it happened, but we might know *how* it happened. Perhaps we stopped dreaming. Maybe we suspended our belief in the goodness of God. Somehow we stopped letting our small sticks set sail. We stopped trusting the wind to get us to the other side, and we settled for life on the surface rather than finding it in our depth. The reason for this is simple. Going deep can be scary. Remembering some of the snapshots in this book has unraveled me at times. It has been all at once beautiful and painful, and I've felt myself sinking more than once.

It's not the first time someone has experienced the same sinking feeling I've experienced, of course. It happened to a man named Peter when Jesus invited him out on the water. He stepped out on the surface of the water, but he didn't stay there long. It wasn't on the surface where Peter found his need for Jesus; it was only when he started going a little deeper that he became desperate enough to call out to God for help. The same is true for you and me.

I don't want to live life on the surface anymore. I'm willing to bet you don't, either. The thought occurred to me that some of these reflections might sink me if I wrote them down, because then I'd need to deal with them. I also realized the greater possibility that calling them out just might save me. When I hesitated, I reminded myself that it's in the sinking where we find our rescue. Like Peter, it's getting beneath the surface that lets us realize our absolute need for a Savior.

There's another version of ourselves that lies some-where under the surface. It's the one shaped and scarred by tremendous joy and painful loss. It is equally us, it's just a different version. This version of ourselves is not one we're accustomed to letting people see, because it resides in the recesses of our lives. It takes time and energy and moments of deep reflection for us to see this version of ourselves. It's not the depth that blocks our view; it's the clutter on the surface that does. It's our instinct to flee, to escape pain rather than confront it. But it's in the engagement that we continue to grow.

It's been a while since I've been back to that pond. I knew if I went back and took a good hard look, I'd expect to see a much older version of me, but I'd also hope to see a wiser one, too. There have been many changes in my life over the years. Perhaps the largest one has been that I'm no longer looking at the reflection on the surface to under-stand my life, my faith, or anyone else's. I've been looking a little deeper.

The stories in this book are what I've found out about my own life. They're in no particular order; they're a scrap-book full of snapshots, not an encyclopedia about my life. They include both joy and pain and everything in between.

I've learned that we each need to see what's at the bot-tom of ourselves to understand more fully what everyone else sees on the surface. This book is my attempt to find my way back to the pond again, to look into it a little deeper and see a reflection of Jesus instead of just seeing all of my failings and flaws. It's also a standing ovation to all of you who have had the guts and the grit to return to your own ponds and launch a couple sticks across it. It's a prayer for those of you who, like me, have taken on a little water on the trip, and it's an invitation for all of us to lean in over our lives and begin to see ourselves the way Jesus sees us.

The pond isn't just the surface or the bottom. You aren't either. Most of what makes it up lies somewhere in the middle—between the clutter on the surface and the depth of the bottom. This is the exact spot where Jesus continues to stand in all of our lives. Right in the middle.

It's where love lives.

CHAPTER 1

The Lodge

We've changed a lot since the night the Lodge burned down.

It's odd how much I still remember about that night. It makes me wonder if God spends much time thinking about who we were and all of the details surrounding the difficulties we've experienced in our lives. I know He could remember everything if He wanted to, but I can't help but wonder if He thinks that the fires we've endured don't matter as much as the future He's promised us. Certainly God uses everything in our lives; nothing is wasted. But among His favorite questions for us isn't where we've been and what we've been through, but "Where do we go from here?" Like the disappointments we've all experienced, what stands out in my memory of the fire are just a few snapshots. The phone call, the family gathered close, standing next to the charred foundations, and the smell of smoke. I think God wired a lot of us to remember just a few parts of our pain, because He knows we don't need all of the details to remember the lessons we've learned.

We're making plans to rebuild the Lodge one step at a time. We don't know for certain what it will look like, but my bet is that it's pretty close to what we had. It was a bad day for us, to be sure, but not as bad as it was for Lloyds of London who insured the Lodge against fires. It could have been so much worse. Our agent said in jest they'd insure us again if we promised not to have any matches or fireplaces or stoves or careless painters on the property.

Nothing remains of the Lodge. The intensity of the fire even destroyed the foundations. That takes a lot of heat. But you know what? I'm kind of glad it did. If there were even one old charred beam still standing after the fire, I'd be tempted to use it to rebuild.

We do this all the time in our personal lives, too. We keep scorched pieces from our biggest failures and incorporate them into our lives as we rebuild ourselves. It's not a good construction practice with wood, and it doesn't make for a good future when we do it with our lives, because it only reminds us of our past. Sometimes we're best served to start all over. This takes getting the foundations out, too. This doesn't mean we get rid of our faith; far from it. We do this because sometimes God wants us to rebuild our lives from scratch. It's what I've done a couple times.

Maybe you have, too. We start over in our lives the same way we'll start over at the Lodge—we'll make it a holy place again, nothing more and nothing less. Sometimes getting there requires clearing absolutely everything away from what we had, or who we were. Doing this is both simple and hard, yet we all get to decide whether we'll do what is required. And for the courageous at heart, we simply start again.

When we've suffered loss, starting again always feels like a gamble. Will we risk it all, knowing it might all just burn down again? Each of us has to decide if we'll ante up and play another hand, or push away from the table and call it a day. I don't think God gambles. He doesn't need to. He sees the future and because He does, He already sees the beauty we've yet to find in the rebuilding. He doesn't just make beauty from the ashes; He makes something far better. He shapes us into who we're becoming.

Sure, we could fill in the charred hole where the Lodge once was. We could make a sand volleyball court or put in a deck and some picnic tables. We could make it look like there was never a loss there. I've done that in my life more than a few times. We asked our grown kids what they wanted to build in the place where the Lodge used to be and with one voice they said they wanted to rebuild it. We all wanted back what was lost. It's a question worth asking for each of us, after we've had a setback or two in our lives, whether they are big or small. Do we want what we've had, or do we want something different for our lives? Sometimes different isn't better—it's just different.

The Lodge is a place we built in Canada, which has become a place of rest for all of us. It isn't the easiest destination to visit. In fact, it's pretty difficult to get to. The only way in is by boat or seaplane. There are no roads or power lines or water lines for a hundred miles in the shortest direction and a thousand miles in the longest. We make our electricity from a river, which carries the snowmelt off of a glacier on the property to the edge of the ocean where we live. We get our water from one of a dozen waterfalls on the property. We grow vegetables in our gardens and catch fish and crabs from the ocean inlet behind the Lodge, which is more than a thousand feet deep. The only reason Bob ever flies out of the inlet to the store is to fill up on ice cream and Pop-Tarts. I know. Don't judge him. Our only neighbor for ten thousand square miles is the Young Life camp next door called Malibu.

This part of the world is beyond beautiful. The azure sky, snowcapped mountains, giant cedar trees, and miles of far-reaching inlets are unlike anything I've ever seen. Photographs don't capture the magnitude of pure beauty. The mountains on our property start at sea level and soar to over ten thousand feet in some places. At our home in San Diego, we discover a seagull or two and are wowed. Up at the Lodge, there's a forest full of animals. Bears, bald eagles, and baby seals are common sights, and it's not unheard of for a pod of orcas or a gray whale to make a silent and grand appearance.

We bought this property years ago, and it's been our life's work to build a place where people can come and get the rest they need. We've deed-restricted thousands of acres of forest in the inlet so they can never be commercially logged. Most of what we don't own is known as "Crown Land" and will never be owned by anyone but the government of British Columbia. We built the Lodge itself to have dozens of places for people to sleep. We constructed it out of beautiful, huge cedar logs. Each one was hewn by hand in a yearlong painstaking process with a drawknife. Each log perfectly fit to the log below it. Not even an ant could fit through a crack in the massive three-story building.

At the camp next door, hundreds of high school and college volunteers spend their summers serving the thousands of high school students who come to Malibu as campers. These volunteers wash dishes, clean toilets, cook, and mow lawns at the camp. With very little sleep, they try to make each week for the campers the best week of their lives. What I've always liked most is how they show God's love by what they do more than what they say. The campers aren't the only big winners; the volunteers are too. They develop friendships and make memories, which will last them a lifetime.

A dozen or more times each summer, we invite all of the camp volunteers to come over to the Lodge. We fill them up with cookies, iced tea, banana bread, and hugs. But our real joy is to see them find some well-deserved rest. I've lost count of the exact number of people we've welcomed into the Lodge, but it's been thousands. It's hard to take a break on a day off at camp if you can still hear and see others working hard. So, we invite the volunteers over to come aside and rest. The Lodge is a place to leave our shoes at the door, curl up on dog beds, leather sofas, and overstuffed chairs. It's a place to take the time to stop and breathe.

Because we know what we had, what we lost, and what we want, we'll start again. We'll cut the logs, stack them high, and fill the new Lodge with new memories. We decided there's not much we'd want to change this next time around. Maybe we'll put in a couple fire sprinklers, but who knows. While I'm not certain about all of the details of the reconstruction, here's what I know we'll do. We'll build something that will serve who we've become, not just repeat who we were. The biggest mistake we could all make in our lives is to rebuild things we've outgrown or to live in constant fear that we might lose what we have all over again. It won't be the fires that destroy our lives and our faith. It will be obsessing over not getting burned again that will.

Early on, I thought it was a little strange when people described Jesus' message as "good news" when what Jesus actually said is if we followed Him we'd suffer loss. Tremendous loss. A lifetime full of it. More than we can ever imagine. Painful, searing, dream-crushing losses. He said if we did it right, it would eventually even cost us our lives. If that's the good news, it kind of makes you wonder what the bad news is. There will be people we put our confidence in who will fail us. There will be relationships which should have gone wonderfully right, and they will go horribly wrong. What I'm learning is that the good news in our faith isn't found in avoiding the pain, but in living through the loss, walking through the ashes, and stacking the logs once more knowing they could burn down again. What has been growing inside of me is a confidence that whatever it is we put our efforts into, it's God's, and He can do whatever He wants with what we build in our lives.

We have a routine before heading up the inlet every summer. It's been the same whether we had a Lodge there or a pile of ashes. The transition to get up to Canada always includes a lot of planning and packing and filling a landing craft full of food, supplies, and clothes. Some people are good at transitions. I'm not. My best excuse is that I am a nine on the Enneagram scale. Apparently, nothing sucks the life out of nines more than transitions. Moving from place to place pushes all the wrong buttons inside of me in just the right order. Still, I know what it's meant to our family to spend our summers together in Canada, so I'm happy to do the work. I'm willing to leave places I love to be with people I love more. I wonder if Jesus felt a little the same leaving heaven to be with us.

Arrival day in Canada means unpacking and storing everything and then assessing just how harsh the winter was on the property. There are always a few broken branches on walkways and in flowerbeds, pine needles in the rain gutters, and loose rocks that have fallen on the roads. We affectionately call doing all of this work "waking up the Lodge." While none of it is easy work, it's good for the soul. We all need to wake ourselves up once in a while, too. To take a good look at what's accumulated in the seasons of our lives and deal with it. Oftentimes I don't want to do this. You may not want to, either. But, we need to do it anyway. Don't be afraid to roll up your sleeves and move some of the debris or knock down the cobwebs that have amassed in your life and your faith over time.

This year, when we packed to leave for Canada after the fire, I wasn't sure what we would need. On the one hand, since we lost almost everything, it was pretty easy to figure out what should be on the list to bring—everything.

On the other hand, it wasn't easy, because what we really needed was to go and be sad and grieve for a while. I didn't know how to pack for that.

A number of years ago, we had built a small house just down from the Lodge and named it the Writer's Cabin. It's hard to believe, but almost a decade after its construction, we had never spent the night there. A few friends have stayed there over the years to work on songs or write books, but we would only visit to drop off cookies and check in on them to make sure the slow writing process hadn't killed them. Now, without the Lodge, it was our time to move in there. What we found when we got to the cabin was that it had everything we needed. There were a couple plates, some silverware, and a trustworthy coffee-pot. We were reminded again about the beauty of simplicity in our lives. These lessons often come at a staggering personal cost but are worth every penny.

We have friends who live on the Lodge property year-round. Some people would call them caretakers, but they're much more than that to us. Thankfully, Paul and Dorothee were in one of the other buildings on the property when the fire happened. Losing the Lodge was hard on them too. They led the original crew who built it. After the fire, they thoughtfully helped haul away most of the charred debris. It was a miracle that the fire consumed the Lodge and left everything around it intact. There were fuel tanks with thousands of gallons of aviation fuel, diesel and gas less than one hundred feet from the fire. If the tanks had gone up in flames, so would the entire forest. I call it a miracle. I am not exactly sure how angels work, but I keep imagining a team of them, covered in soot, standing shoulder to shoulder with singed wings keeping the fireball from destroying the forest and surrounding buildings.

Each time we walked past the crater where the Lodge used to be, we hauled away a little more of the charred bushes, trees, and pieces of melted metal and glass. Doing it all at once would have been too much for us, but doing it a little at a time was better. I think we're all this way. Most of us can deal with our losses a little at a time. Going slow gave me the time to find an object buried in the dirt, pull it out, and try to figure out what it used to be. For some reason I don't fully understand yet, I needed to identify each of the things I found before I could get rid of them. Was it part of a light fixture? A piece of the stove? Hardware from a door? I felt a special kinship with one bent and scorched snowman cookie cutter found in the rubble. It was as if we both knew we'd gone through a lot of trauma. I'd stand there, turning each thing I found around in my hands like they were a puzzle piece, until I could figure out what it was and where it had been before everything went up in flames. I think I had to accept what was lost and properly say goodbye as a necessary part of moving on. To a greater or lesser degree, we all need to do this with our sorrow. We have to figure out what it was that we lost and then name it. Even more important than naming it is letting it go. Our motto after the fire became this: "We're sad, but we're not stuck."

———

We got the whole family together at the place where the Lodge once stood and had a small memorial service. We named things we lost, remembered the beauty of the people who had come over the years, and said goodbye to the Lodge that had been a witness to it all. We reminded ourselves that memories aren't flammable and reassured ourselves that there would be more to come. We know these new memories won't replace the old ones, but will stand beside them as silent witnesses to the goodness of God and the resilience hope gives us all.

Every time a wave of emotion hits me, I'm still surprised. Just when I'm feeling a little bit stronger, the tears come and then disappear just as fast. We don't need to understand what we feel in order to experience it deeply. Life can be painful. It's what we do next that becomes who we are. What some of us do is medicate our pain with activities and routines. Some of these serve us well and others don't. Find the ones that help you get more real and do plenty of those. Don't let pain keep you from going to deep places, from doing some work on your hurts so you can get on with the important business of living the rest of your life. Sad is okay, stuck isn't helpful.

One thing about pain is that we don't get to decide when we'll deal with it. When the most severe pain arrives, it demands center stage in our lives. Mine hit the hardest when I was pruning the bushes and trees that had been planted next to the Lodge. I'd pruned and clipped them yearly before the fire. Some of the plants had survived the blast of heat and some didn't. I spent hours apologizing to them for letting this happen. Even odder was the lawn in front of the Lodge, which still stretched out like thick green carpet in front of the now empty space the Lodge had occupied. I watched Bob lovingly mow the lawn because it still needed to be done, and the tears would come again. I quickly realized that these things we were doing weren't random chores; they were our personal offerings.

One day as I walked past the burnt foundations I came upon a deer and her fawn. They had wandered in among the rubble and were standing side-by-side. Their noses were up in the wind and their ears perked as they turned their heads toward me in perfect unison. They looked as confused as I was when the fire happened. *What the heck happened here?* is what their expressions seemed to say. I felt like I'd let them down. I whispered back, "Sorry, guys," then reminded myself that the beauty of the Lodge and surrounding trees would return again someday.

Loss visits all of us. None of us gets to opt out. Rather than praying that I never experience loss again, my prayer has been that God would show me what's possible on the other side of the loss. While we're waiting to find out what God might have for us, we might be sad for a while but we're not going to be stuck. We're going to move forward. Love keeps us going and hope moves our feet.

I'm not much of a basketball player, but if I was, I wouldn't let the fact that I had missed a shot keep me from taking the next one. Don't let the fear about what you've lost keep you from risking and reaching in your life. Here's the question I think God asks all of us at some point: What's your next step? None of us know what God might do next, but we get to decide what we'll do next. Get back in the arena. Press into the pain. Find new building materials and get back to your life.

The fire might have taken the structure and all of our belongings and precious treasures. Even so, God didn't burn our Lodge down to show us His power. He didn't need to. He had already wowed us with our family and friends a long time ago. What I think God does is to allow each of us to go through difficult times to show us His presence through it. It's as if He reminds each of us in our most difficult circumstances that the most beautiful waterfalls only happen in the steepest places in our lives. Every time I would look at the gaping hole where the Lodge once stood, I reminded myself that love *still* lives here. Because love doesn't need a building, and it never has—it just needs us.

CHAPTER 2

Meeting Bob

When I first met Bob, I had just left rehab and there was a warrant out for my arrest.

The warrant wasn't so bad. I had a glove compartment impressively crammed with unpaid parking tickets. The city couldn't let it slide anymore. The reason I was in rehab wasn't so benign. It was actually the result of a lifelong buildup of unresolved pain.

Insecurity is a funny thing. It makes us into someone we're not as a way to cope with someone we used to be. For me, it started at home. Growing up, my dad had been critical of my mother's weight, and he evidently didn't want my sister and me to look like her. One day my dad called us into the bathroom. He was standing by a scale he had placed on the floor with his arm extended, inviting us to step up. I can't remember the number that appeared, but I remember being so humiliated. This was another moment for me. I began to believe the lie that the love and acceptance and approval I longed for was conditional and depended on my outer appearance. This happened in high school, but when I left for college this untruth found a corner of my suitcase to hide in. When I unpacked my clothes in my dorm room, I unpacked the lie too.

My first experience with high school parties and boys was motivated by my need to numb the constant, searing pain of insecurity. I would go to Friday night football games and shyly follow the "in crowd" to the big party afterward. I would meet boys and recklessly date them. Without words, I would beg them to fill the vacuum I felt, to give me a cheap reprieve with their affection. It never worked, of course, and all of this left me with feelings of guilt, regret, and more unspeakable pain. Each trip down this battered path was like ripping the Band-Aid off the wounds in my life. Predictably, my poor choices made me feel like a walking collection of wounds.

With the increasing stress and anxiety I felt each day, I began to suffer from constant stomachaches. By the time I was nineteen, I regularly took laxatives. My body quickly became addicted to these pills. For years I had accumulated lies and hurts inside me like a hoarder. I wasn't only reliant on the laxatives to give me physical relief, I got addicted to the emotion that came with feeling "empty."

My physical health was rapidly deteriorating, my periods had stopped, and I wondered if I would ever be able to have children someday. I knew I wanted my life to mean much more than it had. I knew I would need to be healthy physically, mentally, and spiritually if I ever wanted to get there.

One day during class, my professor made an announcement that the school was offering free counseling for anyone who wanted it. He asked if anyone would be interested. I looked around the class and everyone else did too. I knew I was in trouble and needed help, but my arm felt like it weighed more than all of the rest of me. In one of the most courageous acts of my young life, I raised my eighty-pound arm in the air. The teacher had not been subtle, but I was desperate enough to not care. The pressures in my life had created a perfect storm, and I was willing to grab on to anything that might float.

After receiving a sliver of light from the free help, I was flipping though the channels in the studio apartment where I had locked myself away. The news that night featured a local hospital treating people for addictions and eating disorders. I made an appointment to meet with the director of admissions to determine which program would help me the most. On the outside I looked fairly normal; I always had a small frame. But on the inside, I knew I was quite sick. Talking to one of their counselors, it was clear that they could help me get better. After a number of meetings with the director, a doctor, and a counselor, I admitted myself into the eating disorder program.

I drove home and packed a few things in a suitcase. I felt like I was running away. And you know what? I was. But I was also running toward something. It was my flag-in-the-sand moment. I declared to myself that I was worth getting healthy again. Because I lived alone, there was no one to take care of my pet goldfish, so I picked up my suitcase with one arm and walked out the door with my goldfish and bowl under the other.

I got to the hospital to check myself in. I met a grumpy nurse on guard at the front desk. She suspiciously eyed me and the goldfish under my arm. "You're not going to eat that, are you?" she said in a snarky tone. Honestly, the thought had never crossed my mind.

I still had a little sass left in me and snapped back, "Do you think it would help? Do you have a cracker?" I knew in that moment I was going to be okay.

I will be forever grateful for that time of healing. I came out the other side a lot more clear about the things that were important to me and the direction I wanted to go. My faith was rekindled. Once again I was reminded of God's faithfulness. I started to see myself the way He always saw me. I could believe for the first time in ages that even with all of my problems and shortcomings, God thought I was beautiful.

It wasn't long after that I met Bob. Poor guy.

––––––––––

Of course, it took me a while to open up to anyone about these experiences, and I presented my newfound self as authentically as I could muster. I knew I was still a work-in-progress, but I had rolled up my sleeves and for the first time I was doing the work.

When we first met, Bob had it bad. I mean, really bad. I still don't get how some people are wired that way. From what I could see, he was head over heels about me and we'd only been in the same room twice. Both times were only for a couple minutes, maybe less. Unfortunately, as I'm sure you can imagine, I wasn't really looking for a relationship and was taking a much-needed break from dating. It's funny how God often takes us to a place where we've gotten to the end of our rope before He hands us another one and helps us tie a new knot.

Bob was persistent to the point of being pesky and kept asking me to go to one place or another with him. I waved him off as politely as I could, but he just didn't seem to get it. The guy was in law school, so I figured it wasn't that he didn't understand what "no thank you" meant. I think he just kept choosing to forget that I had said "no thank you."

I finally gave in to an invitation he made to have dessert together. It sounded innocent enough, and I thought if I went to this one place with him he might stop asking. When I showed up at his door, he grabbed a grocery bag from the kitchen table and we jumped in his car and headed for a local marina. We walked down to the dock and he explained that he had borrowed a sailboat from a friend. When we got on board, he emptied out his grocery bag. Inside were all of the ingredients to make cherries jubilee.

He went down below and got the alcohol stove going in the galley of the boat. What we soon realized was that the alcohol in the stove wasn't burning completely and the cabin was quickly filling with unignited, vaporized fumes. There were two real possibilities. We could have blown up or passed out. Instead, we managed to make our way up top where the air was clear. We laughed a lot as we recalled the moment we realized something was horribly wrong. Under a beautiful, star-filled sky, we sat on the deck and ate cold cherries out of a can. The food was far from perfect, but the night couldn't have been better. By the end of the evening, I reluctantly admitted to myself that a different kind of flame had sparked in me. This was the moment I decided not to abandon ship on a relationship with Bob.

Maybe this guy would be worth spending a little more time with.

The next day, with the eagerness of a three-month-old puppy, Bob invited me to go rock climbing with him. I'd seen what he'd done with a stove and a bunch of cherries the night before, and I was curious whether he was any better at climbing than cooking. Rock climbing seemed a little ambitious for a second date. Typically, couples go to the park, see a movie, eat frozen yogurt, or watch a sunset. But this was Bob.

His invitation reminded me about something from my past, a tree near my house that I desperately wanted to climb. The lowest branch was a little too high for me to reach. No matter how hard I tried to jump for the branch, my hands would slip and I'd land right back where I started. My hands and knees got scuffed and bruised, but that didn't stop me. One day I figured out that the banana seat on my bike propped against the tree trunk made a perfect step for me to reach the first branch. I didn't need to ask for anyone's help or permission; I just climbed the tree all on my own. All the trying and falling was worth it for the security that came from being in my tree.

I never questioned my safety in the tree and I didn't need to. There was no rope and no harness. The tree was solid; I knew it would hold me. Trust can be tricky. It's hard to learn to trust if your confidence has been shaken. When we find ourselves clinging to our own cliffs, it's hard to imagine there is something better than what we've been attached to. Something was starting to change inside of me. I decided it was time to reach for the next limb—to take a step forward rather than a step back. I was slowly beginning to think I could trust Bob, boat stoves and cherries jubilee notwithstanding.

Bob picked me up early the next day. He had lunches, climbing harnesses, and a bunch of ropes in the back of his old Volkswagen Bug. There was nothing normal about this second date. It felt different and I liked it. We got to the gorge where Bob said he'd spent some time climbing over the years. I grabbed our lunches and followed him up a narrow path to the bottom of the cliffs. As we got closer, I could see the summit. The sight of it made my stomach turn. I'm not big on heights. It's the same feeling I get every time I drive across a bridge or climb a ladder to change a lightbulb. Staying at the bottom feeling sick sounded like a better alternative to climbing the vertical cliffs that towered above us, but Bob talked me into following him up the hill. I knew his persuasiveness would serve him well someday if he became the attorney he hoped to be. Using some type of secret Jedi move, I'm sure, he made it sound like the whole thing was *my* idea.

We strapped into our harnesses and Bob scampered away somewhere around the rocks. He said he was going on ahead to "top rope" me. I wasn't sure what that meant, but it sounded like it involved me climbing up to him. Fifteen minutes later, I could see Bob leaning over the ledge above me. He threw the rope down and one end landed at my feet. On the end of the rope was a figure-eight knot for me to clip my carabiner into. I could tell he knew what he was doing, which only underscored the fact that I didn't.

The huge grin on Bob's face was in stark contrast to the concerned look on mine. I wasn't sharing his enthusiasm, but I was glad the rope attached to my harness was tied off and firmly in his grip. His voice was calm and confident, even if a little too cheery considering this was the scariest thing I'd ever done. Forget about comfort zones; this wasn't even in the same continent of comfortable.

I called up to Bob, my voice quivering, "I don't think I can do this."

"Sure you can," he said optimistically with a laugh. "Just make one move at a time. I've got you."

I double-checked the buckles on my harness, gave a little tug on the climbing rope, and (with more than a little hesitation) reached up and made my first move. Sometimes that's all it takes. We all start by starting. It's usually the first step that's the hardest. You raise a hand. You admit the problem. You ask for help. You tie the knot. You start climbing. Everything after starting is just making the next move.

As I climbed, I mumbled dryly to myself, "Geeze, it's as if I have to trust this guy with my life." Suddenly, this thought echoed back at me. I could've sworn there was a flash of light too. I looked up at Bob to see if perhaps he saw the flash. For the first time, I felt the truth of this statement sink into my soul. In that moment, I realized what I'd probably suspected the first time I met Bob but hadn't allowed myself to fully believe. He *was* someone whom I could trust with my life. He wasn't the kind of guy who would ask me to step onto a scale and measure up. He would ask me to step into an adventurous and purposeful life where we could both lead with love.

The breakthroughs I experienced as I climbed that day changed everything. I'd like to say the clouds parted, the sun shined brighter, and little birds with blue silk ribbons circled above my head. Maybe they did. I don't really remember all of the details of the moment. What I know is that I continued to feel a tug on the rope that connected us together, I felt the slack continue to be pulled up, and I kept taking the next step toward Bob. One move after another, I climbed up a scary cliff toward a person who kept saying "I've got you."

I reached over my head to a small crack and pulled myself up as I found a small toehold for my feet. I felt Bob pull up the slack on the rope as I inched higher. There was something reassuring about feeling the rope tighten. "I've got you," Bob called down. I realized Bob actually did have me. If I lost my handhold or my footing, I'd slip, but I wouldn't fall far.

I eyed the next handhold and the next and the next. Each time inching my way a little further up the cliff. I wished more than once I had suction cups attached to my knees and perhaps even my forehead to help hold me to the rock.

It wasn't the strength in my arms and legs but the confidence I found in Bob that kept me going. I knew climbing this cliff would be impossible to pull off on my own. I wouldn't be able to trust my experience because I had none. I couldn't trust my strength because I had little. Instead, I needed to trust the rope, the harness, and a person far above who kept saying the same three words to me: "I've got you." All I could do was reach as high as I could and let my feet follow. I let the words "Just make one move. I've got you" take root in my heart. Without a doubt, that was when I fell in love with Bob.

When I put all of the other distractions out of my mind, the rest of the climb became easier. I kept reaching. Bob kept telling me he had me and I slowly moved up the cliff.

Bob never promised I wouldn't pop off the rock. He just let me know he'd have me when I did. I think he learned this from Jesus. When I finally pulled myself up and over the top edge of the cliff, it felt really good to be standing with Bob at the top of the big thing I'd been on the bottom of a short time before. Our relationship started on the side of a mountain and somehow foretold that there would be many more we'd climb together.

I heard someone describe Jesus as a rock. That afternoon, I found out He's more than that. He's also a rope and a confident voice encouraging me to keep making the next move toward Him.

The Bible talks a lot about trust. I used to think it was something we give, but now I think it's something we both receive and we give in equal parts. Trusting isn't something we achieve merely by agreeing with someone. It's earned through shared experiences. It isn't born out of theoretical needs; it's realized in the crucible of desperate, actual needs and is only really learned in the context of risk and engagement. Checking into rehab, asking for help, raising a hand, or waving a white flag. Trust is the offspring of faith, confidence, and action. Our ability to give and receive trust is the only path leading us to the other side of the insecurities which are blocking our view of our needs.

Someone told me once that trusting God is like letting go. I have a clearer picture of what trusting someone means after rock climbing with Bob. Perhaps letting go is part of trusting, but I think it involves a lot of hanging on too. It means making moves when you can't see all the handholds. It's feeling the slack being taken up on the rope as you climb toward someone you're learning to love unconditionally. It's climbing toward a confident whisper from Jesus saying, "Trust Me, I've got you."

CHAPTER 3

Just Imagine

When our kids were little, they loved making up games and dreaming big ideas into reality. With their imaginations, all they needed to do was think it and it was as if it happened. One time, they imagined the floors in our house were covered in hot lava. Apparently, a volcano had erupted somewhere upstairs—probably in the boys' room, but nobody was really sure. The kids ran down the hall, waving their arms over their heads, telling all of us to run for our lives. They had me convinced, so I ran down the hall waving my arms over my head with them. By the time the lava flow had slowed, we were all safe downstairs in the living room, crouched on top of the sofa cushions. The kids came up with a plan to make their way back to their bedrooms by crossing over the lava without touching it. It sounded pretty risky to me, but I gave them a thumbs-up anyway. Their little hearts soared as I watched them hop from chair to sofa to stair railing without singeing a single toe.

A few years later, we saved up for a family vacation to Hawaii. The kids were still little and had no idea that our hotel was actually built on top of an ancient lava flow. We explained to them that it's how every island was made— Hawaii is just a bunch of lava that cooled. What once created chaos in our home became a beautiful place to enjoy and play in freely as a family. This place was paradise to us. Exotic plants grew everywhere, birds nested, and gentle waves from the Pacific Ocean lapped up against the shoreline. The volcanic eruption changed everything there for a while, but not forever.

Most of us think of paradise as a place where nothing has ever gone wrong. I disagree.

We often find our safest and most beautiful places where the lava once flowed. These are places where we've been able to find the beauty because we're not living in the past anymore. We've not only outgrown it, we've outlived it. It doesn't always happen fast, but it happens. Don't let what's happened in your past stop you from moving forward with your future. Give it some time. We can find our way around the lava where it flowed and build something beautiful on it when it cools. Give it the time it needs, but don't let your pain fool you into believing it's never the right time to deal with it.

I bet one of the reasons Jesus loves children so much is their ability to imagine things. Our kids weren't slowed down by the unanticipated volcano erupting, or the lava flowing like a river through the house. They danced where they had seen the lava once flowing. They figured out the resolution as quickly as they had made up the eruption. They trusted their childlike nature to get them over or around all of the obstacles in front of them. Truth be told, my kids knew they weren't in jeopardy because they had all they really needed. They knew they were loved. What else is there? Their belief in what was possible outweighed any doubt or hesitation they may have felt. The knowledge that they were loved empowered them. Their childlike faith has always inspired me. It's the kind of worldview Jesus talked about a lot with His friends.

In my childhood, I wasn't a stranger to dreaming big dreams and using my imagination. In elementary school, I loved listening to records. I would sprawl out on the floor of my bedroom for hours, playing them over and over again. With my nose close to the spinning record, I watched the needle at the end of the arm roll across the grooves of the album. When the music stopped, I would clean the dust ball from the tip of the needle and carefully replace it between the song I liked and the one I didn't. We all get a chance to do that in our lives if we want to. Stop playing the songs in your lives that aren't pointing you toward your faith and your family. Just because you know the words isn't a good enough reason to keep playing songs you've outgrown in your life.

While listening to the music, I imagined I was in a band. Flat on my back, I'd pretend to play air guitar, or I'd stand up and toss my head around with one eye on the mirror to see my ponytail tossing about behind me while I sang into my hairbrush. I figured all of the really good musicians shook their heads, and I was just certain I had a future on the big stage.

One summer, a few of us in the neighborhood decided to start our own band. We named ourselves "The Mimics." The name was simple and catchy and it wasn't too hard to spell. We mostly lip-synced recorded songs. What we lacked in talent and instruments, we made up for with our imaginations, unbridled passion, and volume. We handed out tickets in the neighborhood to our debut backyard concert and waited anxiously for the big day to arrive.

It was finally showtime, and we packed out the backyard with a few neighborhood kids and our six-pound turtle named Henryetta. We set up a record player as far as the extension cord would stretch. We pegged the volume and played songs off a record from our favorite band called The Monkees. Songs like "Daydream Believer" and "Last Train to Clarksville" blared out of the overwhelmed three-inch speakers. We waved to our fans from our little patio stage and they waved back. I think the turtle even lifted his head to see us. We sang the words we knew and mouthed the rest, shaking our heads to the beat of our air guitars and a drum set made from empty ice cream barrels and a pair of sticks.

We were all a little nervous about whether the people who came would like us. It's still how I feel most of the time. But we didn't see the lava that day. Our band was rocking our way over it. All we needed were our imaginations, a simple plan, and a couple friends. No matter our age, this is how most of our dreams still take wing. Someone has an idea, someone else takes the next step, and pretty soon we're handing out tickets to some neighbors and the family turtle. Kids aren't afraid their ideas won't work, because they're not in a hurry to take the credit if they do. They live in constant anticipation of what might happen next, not in fear of it.

Somewhere along the way, a lot of us misplaced our childlike imaginations and stopped believing we could either get around the lava or build something beautiful on top of it when it cooled. We began to question what was possible and what we're actually capable of. We ran and fell, or tried and failed, or risked and lost. Doubt and fear crept under the door and distracted us from who God made us to be. The disappointments in our lives become like volcanoes, and if we're not careful, we'll just see the lava, not the way over it.

One of my earliest memories as a child is of sitting cross-legged on the floor in a circle in preschool. Our teacher placed a big cardboard box in the middle of the class. We could hear the contents of the box rattling inside as she set it down. It was filled with instruments for us to use for music time. She told us we could each pick out one instrument. In an instant, our polite little circle turned into a dizzying swarm of bodies dashing toward the box in the center of the room. As my classmates pushed past each other to get to the box, my head spun. The sounds of squealing classmates and newly chosen instruments filled the room. Small cymbals, wooden blocks, jingle bells, and tambourines rattled, banged, and clanged. I was so distracted and delighted watching everyone else get their instruments, by the time I reached the box, it was completely empty.

Tears from the rush of disappointment and embarrassment filled my eyes, blurred my vision, and flowed down my cheeks as I made my way back to my spot on the rug empty-handed. The teacher noticed and tried to offer me some comfort, but nothing would console me. A voice in my head I hadn't heard before said to me that I didn't get an instrument because I wasn't good enough to get one. This voice was new to me, yet sounded strangely familiar, like a blending of all of the negative messages that had filled my young life. As I grew up, these false words flowed in my life more often. They spread themselves over me like a wet wool blanket on a summer day, making me feel stifled, like an outsider. I felt like I was the one who didn't deserve to be part of everyone else's joy.

I've heard plenty of people talk about Jesus telling His disciples that the first would be last, and the last would be first. They said it was a good thing to be last and that big rewards came to those who waited. Maybe so, but the problem for me was that it was usually the people at the front of the line who seemed to be doing the talking. It was easy for them to hear the music because they were already holding their instruments. They seemed to already have everything going for them and, honestly, their words were a little hard to swallow when I felt like the kid looking at an empty box.

I suppose what Jesus was actually telling His disciples is that it would be costly to follow Him. He knew the world wouldn't play fair with us and He didn't want us to despair when it didn't. I appreciate that, but on that day during music time, the lava flowed and scorched a path right to me. I felt left out and another deep layer in my personality was being formed right there on the carpet. What I didn't realize then is that the lava would cool, and I could build something beautiful on top of it much later.

Lies are a lot like lava. They slip in under the doors and burn down anything they touch. If we hear enough lies about ourselves, we can lose who we are. We set off new volcanoes every time we repeat those lies to ourselves or to others. In the aftermath, we try to cope with our insecurities by trying to be someone else rather than who God intended for us to be.

It's easy to get discouraged when we see others succeed while we stay stuck, like we were planted in a pot. We overlook our own unique gifts as we crane our necks, looking in everyone else's mirror. We wonder if who we are is enough. Yet still, the mirror held in the strong hands of Jesus reflects how He sees us. His confident voice whispers to us, "I see you. I made you. I love you. We can do this." Our reflection never looks more accurate than when we stop looking at the emptiness of the box and instead gaze into the mirror He holds.

Looking back, I wondered why I've held back in my life.

Why was I timid?

What inhibited me from rushing toward opportunities like they were a box full of musical treasures to help me play my song?

Things can happen in our lives and it's like a switch gets flipped off inside of us and suddenly the world looks so different. A lot of us go through life without ever flipping it back on again. The good and simple news of the gospel is this: God's got the switch. When our weak hands don't have the strength, the strong hands of Jesus help us turn our lives back on again.

We've all experienced volcanoes; not everyone has the ability to see how they become islands of beauty later. Emotional burns, scars, and brokenness don't just go away by themselves. They need some time to cool. While they do, we need to find a way through them and eventually they need to be built upon. It will take a little imagination, but we were born to be curious and brave and dream up ways to get over, around, or through the biggest obstacles. We don't need to run from the lava anymore, but instead imagine what it might become in time.

CHAPTER 4

Keep Your Eyes on Your Own Paper

I wasn't a very good student in school. I tried to hide the fact that I just didn't get what the teacher was saying, but it wasn't long before it was painfully obvious to everyone in class that I wasn't catching on. I was slow to raise my hand, or read out loud, or volunteer answers. I was even slower to turn in my homework assignments, so I usually just didn't. Why bother if I didn't understand it in the first place? It wasn't that I didn't care. It was quite the opposite. I cared so much what my teachers thought of me, I just couldn't bring myself to confirm for them how desperately lost I was in class.

When one of my teachers returned graded papers, mine never looked like the girl's assignments sitting next to me. I could see on her paper how she always had a big red "A" on the top of her homework along with happy faces and exclamation marks. Mine had red pen too, each mark circling one of the multitude of mistakes I'd made. This didn't bother me a little. It bothered me a lot.

I couldn't understand how I could be sitting side by side with someone in the same class, with the same teacher, doing the same work, yet I would utterly fail while the girl three feet away soared. Why wasn't I the smart one? Or if I couldn't be smarter than everyone, at least—why weren't we all the same? How could we get the same assignments, yet our grades would be so different?

I know I shouldn't have done this, but when I got new assignments, I started peeking at the answers the girl next to me was writing down. I compared her paper to mine so I could make mine more like hers. I wanted so badly to be like her. I would hold my pencil the way she held hers, I started sitting in my seat the way she sat in her seat, and I tilted my paper the same way she tilted hers at the exact same angle. I'm not kidding. It was ridiculous to the point that if she had caught a cold, I bet I would have sneezed. But do you know what happened after all of this work? It didn't help me one bit. In fact, if it were possible, I did even worse. What has taken me a lifetime to learn is this: I need to keep my eyes on my own paper.

Theodore Roosevelt nailed it when he said that "comparison is the thief of joy." It will rip us off and steal our lunch money every time. Rather than running away, it just stares us down as it blocks our path forward. Jesus talked with His friends a lot about comparison. He said if we wanted to compare ourselves to someone, we should compare ourselves to Him. I think He said that because He knew comparison would slip under the door like the imaginary lava in our house my kids ran from. Like the lava, it doesn't just dominate the room, it burns it down—with you in it. It whispers to us that we're not good enough or smart enough or talented enough or brave enough. It hisses and bubbles in the hallway and says there's no way around it. But the fact is, comparison is a liar. The way forward isn't over it or through it; it's simply to ignore it completely.

As a kid, I lived for recess. I wasn't just good at it, I was all-pro. If recess was the measure of success in school, I could've gone to Harvard. The only thing I didn't like about playing on the playground was my shoes. You see, in elementary school my parents made me wear ridiculous corrective shoes. They said it would help the arches in my feet. Most kids wore cool-looking tennis shoes. I had to wear awful, brown leather shoes. Embedded in the soles of these shoes were metal plates that forced the arch of my foot to curve as my foot grew. Perhaps they helped my arches, but they also flattened my self-esteem. I felt like Forrest Gump in a skirt.

These shoes weren't just ugly, they were heavy too. Imagine what a deep-sea diver in a bell helmet might wear to explore a shipwreck. Those were my shoes. I was drowning in self-consciousness. The only redeeming virtue of these shoes was how much further I could kick a ball than anyone else. Because of this, I was usually one of the first ones to be picked for the team. Without fail, everyone moved back a few steps on the field when it was my turn to kick. I hated the shoes, but for the first time I experienced what acceptance felt like. And you know what? I liked it. A lot.

At the end of fifth grade, there was an awful, yet predictable, parent/teacher conference. I sat outside the classroom door on a wooden bench for what seemed like hours. When my parents emerged, their long faces telegraphed what I already suspected. They told me I was being held back and needed to take fifth grade all over again. They mumbled something about learning disorders and something else called "dyslexia." My young mind spun. I wondered how I caught it. I wondered if I was contagious. More importantly, I wondered if it was curable.

There I stood in my ridiculous shoes, hearing the news about being held back. I was devastated. For a person already confused by comparison, this was unbearable. Fifth graders are savvy. They know how the system works. I did too. At the end of the year, everyone is supposed to move up one grade, not stay in the same one. My parents said they would move me to another school so no one would need to know. I knew they meant well, but this just underscored my embarrassment and created a dome of silence around the fact that I was both flat-footed and dumb. I had failed. Big time. It was another moment.

I changed schools, but I felt like a fraud when I tried to make friends the next year at the new school. I wasn't who they thought I was. I wasn't even who I thought I was. I guarded my secret like I was in the CIA. I didn't let on to even the best of my new fifth-grade friends that I was a repeat customer. The familiar voice of comparison had me convinced that they would think less of me, when in truth, if I had been honest with them, I would have discovered a new depth of true friendship that can only be found in honesty and vulnerability.

That year I went with one of my new friends to a small neighborhood circus that had set up shop in a nearby park for a week. There were no elephants standing on one foot, no lions jumping through flaming rings, and no trapeze. There were just a couple rusty, dangerous-looking rides and a magnificent house of mirrors. We giggled like school girls as we went inside—because that's what school girls do. We moved from mirror to mirror, watching our reflections change. One made us look tall, another small, and the next mirror made us wide and then narrow again. We laughed at our weird reflections as they changed. Comparison is a little like those circus mirrors. It creates an illusion that delights in playing tricks on us. With enough time, it makes it hard to see who we really are anymore.

The voice of comparison didn't end in the fifth grade. It kept following me. I got married, started raising kids, and then another intruder arrived. It was like a home invasion. This one was called organized sports.

———

I didn't play a lot of extracurricular sports growing up. I wasn't very good at most of them, so I didn't feel the need to sign my kids up, either. We didn't have anything against sports. They looked like a lot of fun, actually. But for our family, they just weren't a big priority. Then comparison knocked on my door once again. This time it was holding a baseball bat.

It didn't take long for me to compare myself to the other families who were dropping their kids off at the baseball field each weekend. I heard how the parents would sit in the bleachers together and have cookouts and tailgate parties. I would hear them talk about the big game and how the season was going for them, and I wondered if I was dropping the ball all of their children were hitting by not signing my kids up for the team.

Our family had found other interests. We spent more time around the water than the track. We traveled some and built more than a few tree forts, skateboard ramps, go-carts, and dollhouses in the backyard. Summers were filled with catching crabs in Canada, not fly balls in center field. We did eventually find something that fit our family as well. We enrolled in karate. We all got white pajamas with different colored belts on them. It was good exercise, I suppose, but I think we were all in it for the pj's.

In what felt like a daring move for us, one summer we signed the kids up for soccer camp. All the parents were invited to watch the big game on the last day of camp. The excitement was nothing less than World Cup status. The game was played next to the local Community Recreation Center, which only had an occasional patch of grass. I'm not sure who won that game; I think everyone did.

At one point, our youngest son went for the ball at the same time our dentist's daughter did. She was absolutely unstoppable until they had a thunderous collision. They both fell, and somehow my son landed on her head. We all ran out on the field. I was checking for bruises and our dentist friend was checking for teeth. Each kid had lots of both, so we lifted them up and carried them off the field like heroes. What we aimed for were activities where comparison took the bench.

If you're someone who spends your free time playing sports, don't make the mistake I did and compare what you do to what we did. You're nailing it like an Olympian. You know your family. Keep up the good work. You should spend your free time doing what lights you and your family up, what frees you up, what works for all of you. Do what makes you the most loving, hopeful version of yourself. If that's baseball, soccer, line dancing, or cage fighting—do a lot of that. The point is simple.

Go be your family, not someone else's.

The thing I'm learning about comparison is that the only way it will leave us alone is if we name it for what it is and then ignore it completely. We could spend our time sorting through all of its lies like clothes at a thrift store, or we can spot comparison coming our way, call it a liar, and simply refuse to make eye contact with it.

Low self-worth makes our eye wander toward other people's papers. If this is you, figure out the return address on the messages you're listening to. Jesus is more interested in who we're becoming than who we were. He doesn't want us to become like each other; He wants us to be like Him. The problem is that we're letting other people do that talking for Him. We all have something we are good at. Figure out what it is and celebrate it. Value what you're good at and you'll understand more about yourself. Find your worth and you'll find your release from comparison.

Wanting to be a better version of you is worthwhile. Desiring to change is maturity. Hoping to be someone else is just wasting your time. To the corporate executive who wants to be a sculptor, go get some clay. For the astronaut who wants to play the banjo, take a lesson or two. For the athlete who wants to sing opera, or the musician who wants to be a chef, go learn those things. And to the couples who want to make a career out of raising a family, go adopt or make some people. We don't need a plan to be us, and we don't need permission either; we just need to begin.

We learn self-acceptance when we've experienced total acceptance. Go find someone or something that will love you back with no strings attached and you'll stop comparing yourself to anyone else. It won't be a program or a self-help book or a career that will be our guide to experience the kind of love and acceptance we all crave; it will be a person. For me, it was Jesus. We weren't created to fit in; we were made to stand apart.

God stretches each of our lives before us like a canvas. He hands us the brushes and the paint and asks us to make our lives look like our unique version of His love. Pick your own colors, not someone else's. He only creates originals, not copies, and expects no less from us. Sometimes it's hard to accept that we're enough, right where we are. However, it doesn't make the statement any less true. Let's carry this knowledge deep in our souls and start acting as confident about God's ability to uniquely craft and release love in our lives as He is.

Wouldn't we all like to be more popular or accomplished or talented or notable than we are? Maybe yes and maybe no. We've all spoken to someone who has been there, and they usually say it isn't all it's cracked up to be. The reason is usually the same. They didn't feel like they could be themselves anymore. I've never met one person who liked faking it for very long. Will you fail at a couple things you try as you figure out who you are and who you're becoming? Of course you will. Don't worry about it. Keep at it. Look beyond yourself. Think about living a life full of windows, rather than a house full of mirrors.

We're not our platforms or our positions; we're His people. Each of us is created in the image of God, not as a carbon copy of each other. We don't need to look like each other, act like each other, or be like each other. We need to become more like Jesus. If my hunch turns out to be true, someday we'll all stand before God, and when we do, there will be no need for any more windows or mirrors. Instead, I can imagine Jesus holding a simple carpenter's picture frame around each of us and saying, "I see you. I love you. You are enough, because I am enough."

Until that day comes, I'm going to keep my eyes on my own paper.

CHAPTER 5

Reverse Economy

I grew up near Pasadena. It's a beautiful residential community just outside of Los Angeles. By the time I was born, most of the orange groves had been replaced by subdivisions and parking lots. It's hard to believe there was a time when they were actually trying to talk people into moving to Southern California, but someone came up with the idea of having a parade on January first each year to show off the place they advertised as always being sunny, even when it was the dead of winter in most other parts of the country. Evidently the marketing worked, because the highways now move slower than the parade.

They called this event the Rose Parade. It wasn't long before college football and T-shirt companies got on board with the idea, and the Rose Bowl was born. New Year's Day is a celebration of rest, new beginnings, and football for many people. To me and most of my friends, it was always just about the Rose Parade, and the parade was always about the floats.

What makes the Rose Parade so unique is that each of the floats is decorated entirely with natural flower petals, grass, and seeds. No artificial surfaces are allowed. They literally make these floats by hand, one petal at a time. To cover just one square foot of a float requires so many flowers, a bucket of glue, and a lot of patience. No two floats are alike; it's the diversity of creative expressions that spreads joy all over the world.

Growing up, I would wake up early each New Year's Day and watch the Rose Parade move slowly down Colorado Boulevard on the television. Marching bands would march, baton twirlers would do their twirling thing, and the Rose Queen and her court, sitting on top of one of the floats, would wave to the kids.

When I was in high school, a few friends and I put our names in the hat to be the Rose Queen. None of us really expected we'd make the cut; it was just something to do one afternoon when school was out. After quite a few interviews over the next several months, they picked seven girls to be on the court and after a long weekend together with the organizers, the queen was chosen. It was a long time ago, and I haven't told many people, but somehow they picked me to be the queen that year. I thought with this boost in status I'd get out of some chores at home, but sadly it didn't work out that way. I would have tried to get my little brother to call me "Your Majesty" every time I walked in, but I didn't have a little brother, so I was left to rule over the family cat who was also indifferent about the whole thing.

We all have ambitions. Some are big and some are small, and a couple things you just do along the way for fun. Our big goals will change over time, as will the small ones. The routines we follow in our lives are what enable our goals or impede them. I knew what my goal was for a long time, and it wasn't to sit on top of a float. That was just one of those fun diversions with a couple friends that happened along the way. My biggest goal was to be a wife and mom. When this became important to me, I didn't know who I would marry and I didn't even know if I could be a mom. None of us do, until we find out we're going to become one. It's a reminder to me that we don't need all the facts about our lives to have beautiful dreams about them. The reason is simple. We all build our lives one petal at a time.

Becoming a wife and mom wasn't what my friends were aiming for when I was young, and it isn't the ambition of a number of my friends even now. To them, I suppose it sounded boring and old-fashioned. Who knows, maybe it is old-fashioned. In college it made me wonder if there was something a little wrong with me. I didn't want to run a corporation or sing like a thousand angels, although I can't lie, being able to sing would be cool. I wanted the chance to be a wife and a mom in a way that I had not seen before. Deep down I knew it could be done differently.

There are many amazing women who are literally changing the world as they pursue their chosen paths. You may be one of them. I used to be a little self-conscious and wonder if they would be disappointed to hear about my big ambition. Perhaps they'd think I was small-minded or naive or old-fashioned. What I didn't know then was that there are incredible women in business and incredible ones who aren't. There are gifted women championing important causes and other gifted women who aren't. I've discovered that both women and men can choose to make their greatest lifework creating families at home. Just like the important things these friends of mine who took another path were making, raising a family can literally change the earth as well. It's not a "second-best" thing to do, anymore than it is pursuing a big and beautiful career is.

Finding role models who provided me a target for my ambition was difficult. As a college student, none of the women who were receiving public affirmations were moms. No one said to me that my ambition wasn't a worthy one; somehow I just didn't find a safe, even footing to see my ambition as a noble endgame. I wondered sometimes whether I was aiming low. I had heard a couple women describe themselves as "just" a mom. I thought you had to do other things in addition to being a mom to live a meaningful life, like curing polio. Maybe that. But "just" being a mom? Over time, though, as I came to understand more about how God had uniquely wired me to be, I realized that far from aiming low, what I was aiming for was actually high. It was my own bull's-eye. I like how God makes us different like this. He sees how we love Him and how we love each other as important. I bet it brings Him tremendous joy to see us have goals and ambitions, which are constantly changing. He wants them to be His ambitions expressed in our own lives. All the while, He quietly hopes we'll be His and He will be ours no matter what we happen to be doing.

I place a high value on the degree I eventually earned, and I've never been afraid of hard work. I've had some great jobs and a couple horrible ones too. I've worked in restaurants, in retail, and at an advertising agency. Bob and I flipped houses before they made television shows about people who did this. I've decorated everything from a fancy Washington, D.C., home we fixed up on Capitol Hill to Southern California yachts. Those were fun jobs and flowed from my abilities, but they were not my ambitions. It's good to know the difference between the two. Ability is what we can already do; an ambition is who we want to become.

I've had some lousy jobs too. I did telemarketing research for a local radio station, repainted old rental apartments, and I'm more than a little embarrassed to admit to having spent part of a summer after high school in Hawaii selling crochet bikinis on the beach. I know. Don't ask. I'm mortified to admit it. It's the horrible jobs that get us ready for the better ones. They help us sort out what we're able to do from what we were meant to do. What I've come to realize is that all of these varied experiences got me ready for my favorite work, which has been being a wife to Bob and mother to our kids.

When the kids were young, Bob was home a lot. Now he gets to travel a lot. He's always on the move. It's like he's in the witness protection program. He's like the wind. No one sees him come and no one sees him go. Sometimes, not even me. While we go about what we do with our lives in different ways, the important things we want in life are the same. Family, faith, love, purpose, respect, and joy, to name a few. I get asked every now and again to give advice to young women for their lives. As a rule, I don't give any advice. Everybody has an opinion. What I will pass along is what I've observed in my own life and it's this: I try to focus my time on doing things that serve and advance the most lasting and beautiful of my ambitions. The kind Jesus talked to His friends about. Figure out what those are for you, and do more of that.

Bob and I have a lot in common, but we have our differences too. One of our biggest differences is how we engage the world. He's all gas and no brake. He's a "do-er" and is energized being around people. His favorite number of people to be with—is more. I, on the other hand, am a "be-er." I'm content to spend the afternoon with just a few close friends or family. I'm quiet and prefer not to be in a lot of crowds.

We've found beauty in our differences. Bob travels all over the world doing good and chasing bad guys. My focus is on being home and keeping an eye on homeland security. For a long time, I felt like my ambition was somehow a little less noble than his. After all, he goes to Iraq and Mogadishu, Somalia, and opens schools and safe houses and gets innocent young kids out of jails in Uganda. I go to the store and get the groceries. He meets with sultans and talks about ending wars. I cut flowers for vases around our home.

What used to be unsettling for me, now gives me great comfort. That's how the reverse economy of Jesus works when we let it. I realize that God made us different individually so we could be better together. When Bob travels, I stay home because it keeps both of our lives anchored. We have a family, neighbors, a home, and a life to maintain. Both his efforts for others and my efforts at home are equally important to us. When Bob's not traveling, he t and nurture he needs to reset and recharge so he can continue his efforts around the world. On a parallel track, our family enjoys the continuity I provide because I'm around.

→ Here's the thing. I'm not trying to be like Bob, and he's not trying to be like me. We're each trying to be like Jesus. God didn't make us the same, so we're not trying to act like we are. I think that's where sometimes people get confused and a lot of tension enters into their relationships. If you feel like your ambition isn't big enough because it's not the same ambition someone you love has, don't buy the lie and change who you are. Don't screw it up by trying to change who the person you love is either. Celebrate the differences. Laugh about them. Work with them. End up at the feet of Jesus with them. In God's reverse economy, He makes our differences our strengths so long as He's the one we're all aiming to be like.

Bob brings fun and adventure and risk and spontaneity to our marriage. I give stability, predictability, and a home life for everyone to return to. His passion is to make the world a better place for everyone. Mine is to make our family a better place for generations to come. Don't get me wrong, we both want all of these things. Instead of comparing roles, we've each discovered which ones belong to us; and we try to grow into the fullest expression of Jesus through us, within these respective roles.

It doesn't happen often, but our worlds cross when we travel overseas together. Even then, our differences often play to our advantage. When Bob goes to countries in conflict, he brings lots of balloons. When I come, I bring lots of string. Balloons without strings are pretty easy to find. You'll usually find them floating away over a nearby rooftop. All strings without the balloons leave you looking like you're going to start a macramé project. Together though, they make for tremendous joy. Like Bob and I, they work pretty good together.

If you're single, find your thing. If you're married, find your thing. Don't become each other; become His. Figure out who God meant for you to uniquely be. If you're a balloon person, get the biggest ones you can find. If you're a string person, learn to tie good knots. Start with the ambitions and desires God has given you and then go take the next step with what lights you up. Fuel it with your faith, not just your energy. It could be in Somalia and it might be at the grocery store. Perhaps it will be both. Whatever it is and wherever it is, do lots of it.

When I took a trip with Bob to Iraq, it reminded me of how good it is to do things together that are outside of our normal rhythms. I can't lie. I had a lot of anxiety leading up to the trip. Thirty miles away from where we arrived, ISIS was literally kidnapping and then selling men, women, and children in cages. The world news was filled with reports

of fighting in the areas surrounding where we were causing tens of thousands of refugees to flee ISIS in Northern
Iraq. Bob had planned to go there to be part of starting
a school with some brave friends who had moved there.
The school is for kids who wanted to continue with their
education despite the armed conflict swirling around them.
One school, one book, one kid, one glimmer of hope glued
down like petals on a float. Living out your ambitions is
figuring out what they are, then doing something about
them one at a time.

After so many hours of flying, the flight attendant
announced that we were about to land in Irbil in Northern
Iraq. The mix of excitement and fear and lack of control
rushed through me. *Here we go*, I thought as I put my book
down and raised the shade on the window to see my first
glimpse of Iraq. I could see the airport in the distance like
a speck of dust on a huge sand-colored canvas. *How can
we be landing?* I wondered. *We're still 25,000 feet above
the airport.* Just then, the plane banked hard to the left and
pitched forward causing my forehead to press up against
the window. *Is this a normal maneuver?* I wondered. I've
never heard of a commercial plane doing aerial stunts. I
turned toward Bob to see if he was concerned too. He
responded with a reassuring nod and a thumbs-up. I've
learned to trust his nod.

The plane continued to bank hard as we corkscrewed down toward the airport directly below us. The airplanes apparently do this to minimize the risk of being hit by bullets and missiles fired by terrorists from the ground. The plane continued to spiral toward earth like Alice falling down the rabbit hole. We landed hard, like a lawn dart. When the plane came to a stop at the gate, I was so grateful to be on solid ground. It didn't matter that it was in a war zone. Any reservations I had of *being* in Iraq had been dwarfed by simply *landing* in Iraq.

The battle with ISIS was as close to us as the outlet mall is from our home. I expected everyone I met to be as uptight as me; but oddly, they were just going about their business. They were doing their jobs, raising their families, and living out their ambitions as best they could. Certainly, they were aware of the fight nearby, but they didn't live like it. They woke up, went to work, made lunches, and waved at their friends on the street when they passed by just like I did where I lived.

I thought about how much I would benefit if I approached every adventure, opportunity, or hard thing with an open heart and mind instead of feeling scared, apprehensive, or hesitant. My typical approach to new things is usually to stand back, insulate myself, and create a protective wall around me and those I love. More recently, I've seen in myself a different approach to life emerging.

What I think I'm seeing is the reverse economy of Jesus at work.

I saw firsthand what the life of a refugee was like. The displacement, the tents, the way they shared their meals, water, heaters, and hope. Two women had delivered their babies while fleeing to this area. Sadly, only one of the babies had survived. I heard stories told by the women of what it was like when ISIS rebels took over their community and how they were forced to leave behind their homes to save their lives. It challenged many of the things I've placed the greatest importance in. Family, security, predictability.

When ISIS came to their homes, they gave them three options. Convert, die, or leave. When they left, ISIS set booby-traps in their homes to ensure they would not try to return. If they did, it would trigger explosions. In a much smaller way, I saw the challenges and traps I had set in my own life. While not deadly, I saw the destructive capacity they had, too. ISIS was their enemy. Pride and comparison and ignorance were mine. I hadn't taken a trip with Bob for a few years. The more he traveled, the more I stayed at home. We loved each other enough to see that what God was doing in each of our lives was different. Rather than pushing back against this, once again, I found a quiet confidence in realizing that he's the balloon and I'm the string.

While in Iraq, I learned of a brigade made entirely of women. Their focus is on homeland security too. These women are mothers, daughters, sisters, and wives of soldiers who were killed in the war. Because they plan well, they make great soldiers. The fact that they're women isn't a liability; it's actually their secret weapon. The men in ISIS are terrified by this female group because they believe if they are killed by a woman, they won't go to heaven. I'm not sure whether they're right or they're wrong, but I have a hunch.

Bob and I aren't at war; we're in love. I see the power and importance in my role. I see the beauty in the contrasts in our marriage between what I do and what Bob does. I saw it when I traveled to Iraq hoping to meet some of the needs of others' lives, and while there discovered that they were actually meeting mine. I wonder if the reason Jesus sent His friends out two by two is so they'd be reminded not to look at each other and their differences but to keep their eyes fixed on Him.

Did traveling to Iraq with Bob make a difference? Yes and no. Iraq already has brave men and women there who love God and know how to love others far better than I have learned to do so far. I think God's still holding out hope for me. I don't think me being there helped all that much, but who knows. I don't know if any of us can ever measure the impact we have on others. Here's where I do know I made a difference. Bob and I took a step together. While it was uncomfortable for me, it was great for our marriage and it was greater for my faith. It was like putting one more petal on the float.

When our kids were really young, we took them up to the place where the Rose Parade floats were being made a few days before the event. They didn't know I had sat on top of one of the floats so many years earlier. It didn't matter to them or to me. Each of the kids glued a petal or two on the float. You know what's crazy? When each of the kids was done, they felt like they'd made the whole thing. They hadn't, of course, but what they did do was contribute. Sure, what they had done was as small as one flower petal, yet it was huge to them. They were no longer spectators, they were participants. They were part of adding just a little bit to the beauty. It's what we all can do if we choose to. We do it in our friendships, in our marriages, and we do it every time we find confidence in being who God made us uniquely to be.

Most people I've met want to help others, but they don't know where to start. I'm right in there with you. We all don't need to do big things, but we can do equally important small things. The message of freedom from Jesus to His friends can be boiled down to this: We don't need to build the whole float. Every morning, God gives us a reassuring nod. He lets us know He's with us whether we blow up the balloon or tie the string, and He invites us to add just one more petal to what He's doing in the world.

CHAPTER 6

The Gold Mine

A few years after Bob and I were married, he told me he owned a gold mine. I laughed and told him that was great, because I owned a shuttlecraft and maybe I could park it there. "No really," he insisted. "Honestly, it's up in the Sierra Mountains and it's been passed down in my family for generations."

"A gold mine? We have a gold mine?" I asked a second time from under the sink where I was trying to fix a clogged pipe in the small apartment we lived in. I've always had a little bit of Missouri in me, so I dared him to show me.

A few years later, we drove up to the mountains to take a look at it. This was gold-rush country at the turn of the century in California, and it was fascinating watching the towns grow smaller the further into the mountains we drove. Eventually, we turned down a small road and drove until it ended and then walked quite a way down a small trail toward a river. "We're here," Bob said after we navigated the last steep pitch together. I don't know what I expected to see. Perhaps seven short miners singing "Heigh-Ho," a couple gold pans and a sluice box, or maybe a few picks and shovels. There was none of this.

To my left I saw the entrance to the mine. It was a large dark opening in the side of the mountain just wide enough for a guy with a box of dynamite to enter and just tall enough to stand in. There was no sign hanging from a rusty nail saying "Gold Mine," no wooden beams holding the roof in place, and no kerosene lanterns. I thought to myself, this is not how Disney would make a gold mine look. This was no movie set though. With just a few picks, shovels, and a bunch of explosives, these turn-of-the-century miners had simply started digging into the mountain. They didn't care what the mine looked like from the outside. They were way more interested in finding the gold inside than impressing anyone passing by.

This is my prayer for myself and the ones I love every day. I want to be that way with my faith.

When these miners started digging, there was no promise about what they'd find either. Perhaps only more dirt and rock lay beneath all of the dirt and rock. What made them sit by campfires, eat baked beans, and grab their picks and shovels each day was the expectation of finding treasure that would make the reward worth all of the effort.

I had studied up before the trip and had learned that most of the gold in the area is found locked within a type of rock called quartz. What the miners would do is find veins of quartz on the surface and follow them deep into the mountain, wherever it led them. Their formula for success was pretty simple. Follow the quartz and you'll find the gold.

Just outside of the entrance to the mine was a large pile of earth and rock the shape of a building pad. These were the tailings and spoil left over from all of the digging that had been done. Even though this area was made up of everything unwanted and seemingly had no value, over many years of mining, all of the rock and dirt had made a large flat place where generations later our family could build something. It was yet another reminder to me that nothing in our lives is wasted.

We spent the afternoon exploring outside of the mine. At one point, Bob dared me to go inside, and I mustered only enough courage to peek my head into the darkness. I threw a couple rocks inside but didn't go in. I had read about mineshafts going straight down because this is where following the quartz had led the miners. Looking for gold in someone else's mine is dangerous stuff. Trespassers and claim jumpers do this kind of thing, but it's not a good idea.

I think God had in mind that we'd work in our own mine-shafts. We need to be pretty careful about going uninvited into someone else's. What led someone else to their gold might lead us to disaster.

Outside the mine I looked on the ground for any gold nuggets that might be laying in plain view. As I expected, I didn't find any, but it's always worth a look. I've come to realize that gold is rarely found on the surface around gold mines or in our lives. The good stuff usually takes some digging to get to. While it's sometimes exhausting work, I'm banking on what I saw outside the mine that day. My hope is that the dirt we each move in our lives might actually end up making a wide place for the generations who follow us to build upon.

We're all prospectors in a sense. Our faith is our gold pan and our curiosity our picks and shovels. We can't decide in advance what we'll find when we do the work, but we can decide when we'll start. The best time is usually right now. Will digging deep involve some heavy lifting? You bet it will. Is the outcome certain? Well, yes and no. When we dig in, we'll find a couple things worth keeping, things that are valuable to us and the people we love. You can be certain about that. We'll also discover things we can let go of. This is good but uncertain work. What we let go of are the tailings and the spoil; it's what's left over. Sometimes we need to move a lot of dirt to get to what we find valuable. Keep digging. Remind yourself often that you're not just moving dirt and rock; you're clearing the way for the good stuff. The things that will last in your life and the lives of the ones you love. Nothing is wasted. Move the dirt. Get rid of what's blocking the way. Find your vein, then follow where it leads. The message I bet Jesus would have given to the miners is this: Follow the quartz and you'll find the gold.

During the gold rush, prospectors would often have someone outfit them with what they needed to start looking for the gold. A pick, a shovel, some food. This was called a grubstake. Jesus didn't operate this way. He doesn't grubstake anyone. In fact, He did just the opposite. He told His friends when He sent them out not to bring anything with them. No food, no bag, no walking stick, nothing. All they had was Him. He said that would be enough and it was. The same is still true today.

———————

I first discovered Jesus when I was about eight years old at a summer camp on Catalina Island in Southern California. What I heard about Jesus made Him sound like a really wonderful person. The camp counselors talked about God being a Father to us, and the stories they told about Him each night around a campfire captivated me. I felt like I had found a family where I belonged and had found a Father who accepted and welcomed me just the way I was.

We all want to experience connection. To feel like we're safe and belong and are loved. I liked what I heard at camp. It touched my heart in a way that allowed me to experience the kind of peace, love, and joy I'd only imagined before then. I didn't have the urge to resist or argue or defend what I didn't understand. I experienced the kind of childlike faith Jesus said would be necessary to understand Him. I simply believed that what was being said was actually true. I felt like I had discovered nuggets of gold laying on the surface.

I wasn't raised in a home that talked about God very much. One time I asked my parents why we didn't go to church like the other kids in my neighborhood. It was a simple and honest question, but I got a long, complicated, and confusing answer. Honestly, I didn't follow much of what my parents said, but it had to do with us being agnostics or atheists. I'm not sure if we were one or both. It didn't matter, because I didn't know what either word meant. These could have been the names of baseball teams for all I knew. I supposed that whatever it was that we were, we weren't friends with God. I never brought up the subject again.

During the week at camp, the speaker told us stories from the Bible and talked about Jesus and God and the

Holy Spirit. All three of them sounded great to me. It was like more fun people were inviting me in. I think I liked Jesus a little more than the other two. I was a little concerned that if I said I liked one of them more than the others, someone's feelings would be hurt. I felt like I needed to pick one of them. Kind of like picking a team to be on. It was a huge relief when the camp counselor explained how all three of them were actually one, and I should think of God as my Father. I nodded, but I still didn't really understand. She said it was kind of like Neapolitan ice cream. The three flavors—chocolate, vanilla, and strawberry—made one ice cream. The theology was a little weak, I'll admit. But it made sense to me. I liked ice cream. I liked Jesus. I was all in. I don't think God cringes when we try to explain Him by using metaphors that aren't always very accurate. I think He delights when His kids come home to Him. He isn't worried when we misunderstand a couple things at first; I think He's just delighted when we start.

On the last day of camp, they said that any of us who wanted to invite Jesus into our heart could go on a special trust hike, blindfolded, with our leaders. We made our way up the hill with the leaders guiding the way. I could hear the sound of other campers climbing up the trail above me and boats and seagulls on the beach below. The special place we were heading to was at the top of the hill. We walked in a single-file line, following our leaders' voices as they guided the way. When we got to the top, we took our blindfolds off and we were standing in a circle. In the middle was a cross on the ground, outlined with white rocks. Someone was singing and someone else read something from the Bible. We all prayed and they said my Father who was in heaven was celebrating with us. I cried a deep heartfelt cry that day.

Before we left, everyone was given a little blue scarf we tied around our necks. Truthfully, the scarf sealed the deal. Not only did it look cool, it represented the moment I declared my love for God and began getting to know my heavenly Father. Someone said I "accepted" Jesus that day, but more accurately it felt like He accepted me.

Many years have passed since the time I got home from camp and I've learned a few things. I learned that the Trinity isn't like Neapolitan ice cream and that following Jesus isn't like getting a blue scarf. Instead, it's like getting a pick and a shovel and doing the hard work to get to the treasure.

Back home from camp, I didn't want to unpack my suitcase. I think that I was afraid that if I did, my camp experience would evaporate. My parents told me to unpack my suitcase a couple times, but I just couldn't bring myself to do it. I didn't know how to explain to my parents what had happened in my heart at camp, so I hid my suitcase with my blue scarf under my bed. I didn't think I was being disobedient by not doing what I was told, because in my young and tender heart, I didn't want to risk losing what I had just found. I felt like I'd found buried treasure, and I wanted to hide it deep in a mineshaft.

Eventually, my parents found my suitcase still packed under the bed and I got in a lot of trouble. I was told to wait until my dad got home. I was used to getting spankings growing up, but this one would be different. I think my experience at camp had touched a nerve for my dad. I had returned home changed, and I wondered if his overreaction had something to do with my new faith. That evening, before dinner, I could hear him in his workshop as he cut a paddle with his jigsaw out of a large piece of wood. I knew when he was done he was going to use it on me.

When he came into my room with the paddle in his hand, I started crying and said I was sorry, but it didn't make any difference. Not long after being hit repeatedly with the paddle, deep bruises started to reveal themselves under my skin. The marks on my bottom would last for weeks. At school, I couldn't sit all the way on my desk chair. I had to sit with the bruised side off the seat and hoped nobody asked why I was sitting so weird. My little blue scarf couldn't hide the dark blue bruises on my body or the deeper ones left on my heart.

I was so confused. I had welts from a father who had spanked me and a blue scarf from a Father who I thought would protect me. So I found a mineshaft in my heart and buried all of my feelings and disappointments and hurts deep down inside of it. I decided I wouldn't tell anyone about the pain I had experienced at home or that I had invited God into my heart at camp. It would take me years to be able to talk about either.

———————

Though buried deep, one precious truth I started to understand about my new budding faith was that nothing could separate me from the love of God. Not my parents' unbelief, not a cruel wooden paddle, not the pain, and not even the loneliness.

Our treasure can get buried under our pain fairly easily. Getting to it is hard and messy and sometimes confusing work and we'll make mistakes. One of the most common ones is to start looking for our treasures in other people's mines. When we do this, even if we find what glitters, it's not ours. We can also take on the unsolicited responsibility of digging in other people's mines in the hopes of helping them discover their treasure. Prospecting is lonely work. It's a team sport in some ways, insofar as our friends give us the strength to dig deeper. But at the end of the day, we need to find our own picks and shovels and do the work in our own places.

My relationship with my parents has been estranged for some time now. I realized at some point I can't make them dig for their buried treasures in their lives nor can they help me find mine. All of us know someone who we think has a mine full of undiscovered gold. This side of heaven we'll never really know for sure. Everyone needs to do their own work. Our job is to keep our heads down and tend to our own mines.

It's not always fun to dig deep in family soil. Sometimes we need to move a lot of earth, but the end result is so worth the process. It's the stuff that family legacies are made from; and if we're able to do it well, generations to come will benefit.

The same power that dug Jesus out of a cave can unearth beautiful things in our lives, too. God takes what was once dead, buried, and hidden, and pulls it into the light, dusts it off, and restores every bright and beautiful surface. Follow the quartz in your life and you'll notice the gold in others' lives.

CHAPTER 7

The Jeweler

Some people are jewelry people. I think that's fantastic. The more they wear, the more dazzling they look. Those who pull it off well make it look like it grew there. I'm the opposite.

The feeling of things dangling off my body is just too distracting for me. I feel like a magnet in a metal shop. A small necklace with an outline of a fish feels like an albacore around my neck. Bracelets feel like handcuffs to me. There's probably a name for this sensitivity disorder with lots of syllables I can't pronounce.

It was a really big deal to get my ears pierced on my thirteenth birthday. I was a little afraid of getting my ear poked with a sharp needle. But what made me twitch was the thought of having earrings hanging from my ears for the rest of my life. I was afraid I'd shake my head like a wet dog and accidently poke my eye out. Or worse, I might rip an earring from my earlobe with a hairbrush by mistake. I've heard that hurts a lot.

When Bob and I met and fell in love, I didn't have any reservations about marrying him and spending a life together with all of its challenges. What concerned me the most was wearing the ring, since that usually comes with the deal. I wondered if we could just get matching belts or hats or something. I loved Bob a lot, but I hated jewelry more.

There's a small jewelry shop not far from where we lived. The whole storefront wasn't more than twenty feet wide and was located in the middle of a popular tourist town so there were just enough customers to keep the jeweler in business. We decided to have our rings custom-made by him and called to set a time to meet the following week.

A few days later, we pulled up in front of the jewelry store in our car just as the jeweler and his wife did in theirs. We were a little surprised when he got out of the car slowly. It was obvious the jeweler had been injured. Unknown to us, just a few weeks earlier, a carload of masked men carrying semi-automatic weapons had tried to rob his store. There are two notorious gangs in Southern California: the Crips and the Bloods. From what they pieced together, robbing his store was an initiation rite for a couple of these guys who were joining one of the gangs. The jeweler had some firepower of his own behind the counter and fought back in self-defense. When the gunfire ended, the robbers all got away, but the jeweler had been shot six times. His wounds understandably affected his mobility, and he relied heavily on the cane at his side. One of the bullets had done significant damage to his arm, and one of his hands hung limply from a sling around his neck.

We stood on the sidewalk just outside the store and we tried to find some common ground to break the ice. After a few minutes, he filled us in on what had happened. He said this was his first time back to the store and he'd never been shot before. We said these were our first wedding rings and we'd never been married before. After finding some common ground, I instantly liked him.

With some help from his wife, the jeweler fumbled with his keys, unlocked the door, and pushed past a pile of mail scattered on the tile floor. The air smelled stale with what we thought was a hint of gunpowder. Our eyes adjusted to the dark as his wife turned on a few lights. A plywood board was tacked in place where a glass window used to be. The jewelry case, which had once been full, was still empty. Out of the corner of my eye, I noticed a few bullet holes, which had left jagged divots in the plaster wall. It gave me the chills and I wondered if it was hard for the jeweler to be back in the shop where he had been shot.

The jeweler disappeared in the back for a moment and returned wearing a magnifying visor and carrying a velvet-lined tray with a few diamonds. I could tell every move he made was a struggle, but he was focused. We were his first customers after the robbery and because his hand was still damaged, he asked if we were willing to be patient and accept a ring that might have a couple imperfections in it. His kindness and humility were stunning. Seeing his courage, I let him know if it fit my finger, we were good. What I learned from the jeweler about our rings taught me lessons that would serve me well in my marriage.

What happened to the jeweler might have caused most of us to quit, yet he didn't. Relationships are a lot like that. They involve pushing through difficult circumstances. Taking the next step is the best medicine to recovering when we are feeling less than whole. Will we get it perfect? Of course not. But this brave man found the courage to get back to his work because he created rings that are passed down for generations. We all want to do things that will last. Figure out what those things are and then do lots of that.

Bob has a tendency to rush. I have a tendency to pause. Together we usually get it right. He's taught me how to grab my knees and do a cannonball into a body of water. I've taught him the merits of pausing to check for rocks just under the surface. There's beauty in both. We can waste a lot of time waiting for just the right moment before making our next move. We might pause and wait for the perfect time, or for the tide to change, or for the stars to align. We might want to wait until we feel smart enough, or good enough, or have it all together. The truth is, if you know who you are, to whom you belong, and what you want, your time is now. Like racehorses at the derby, the starting bell has rung; your gate has been flung open wide. It's time to take your next step. Make it a lasting one.

The jeweler made time for us. Even though he was still in physical pain and the shop wasn't officially opened for business, he was still willing to meet with us. There is a quiet power in availability and resolve. None of us know exactly what our challenges or obstacles will be, or when we will face them. The jeweler could have quit, but he got back to his work. Relationships that operate this way find the power it takes to move through the problems rather than linger in them.

We picked out a diamond for my ring. Bob was certainly more than capable of doing all of this on his own; and we could have saved quite a bit of time, but making this decision together made it a better one. It wasn't better because of what we chose, but how we went about picking it. We don't just bring our capabilities to our marriage; we find the joy in bringing ourselves. We're not trying to be efficient with our love, but make the most important choices together.

Designing the ring was one of our first big steps in designing our life together. We were two imperfect people with imperfectly big dreams who loved God. That's about all we had. We knew we would take a few hits in our marriage. We'd taken a couple individually even before we got married. They weren't bullet holes; it might have been easier if they were. Sometimes the invisible kinds of damage we bring to our relationships are the most debilitating. Nevertheless, there is a healing power in taking the next steps together. We thought that building our marriage from scratch would require a lot of big dreams and planning. We found out it was just two people working together, doing what we could with what we had.

We're all deeply flawed people and in desperate need of love and acceptance. In Hollywood, the "here's the ring" moment is usually played out with perfectly polished choreography.

The place is perfect.

The people are perfect.

The jewelry is perfect.

But this isn't a life any of us really identify with. We're all far from flawless, yet love is not expressed by us in perfection, but in how real we are. Committing our lives to one another is less about all of the bedazzling sparkle and more about raw potential and the mystery of two people becoming one. It seemed fitting that as we were puzzling pieces of our lives together, the jeweler was doing the same with his.

There is a beautifully simple formula we've used in our marriage. First, Bob and I figured out what is most important to us. For the two of us, it's our faith. We can't live each other's faith, we can only live our own. Like our rings, our faith comes in different sizes. We're not trying to compare sizes; we're trying to keep it real.

God has a way of turning the world's fables about what a marriage is on its head. We've learned not to take the bait about what marriage is supposed to be and instead focus on who *we* are supposed to be. This took a lot of the pressure off both of us. Engagement wasn't just a period of time before we got married; it was the kind of life we decided we'd lead after we were married. Fully engaged with each other, with God, and with the people around us. We knew we were "generation one" in many ways, and we wanted to become a family grounded in our faith in God and our desire to understand the power of His love in the world.

After a period of courtship, Bob asked me to marry him. I summoned all of my courage as he took a knee and slipped a humble ring on my finger. It was just beautiful. Our new friend, the jeweler, had totally nailed it. It was the perfect ring for us. He had worked in the back room of a musty, bullet-ridden store for about two months. I can't imagine how difficult it must have been. Maybe, like our marriage, there were hard days for him and hopefully easy ones, too. I'm not really sure. When he finally completed the task of suspending a diamond between a few gold prongs, he called Bob in to see the finished product. Unlike the ring, our marriages are never really completed. We work on them for a lifetime and then lay them down at Jesus' feet.

A lot of people get their rings from big jewelry stores. Some have a ring that's been passed down as a family heirloom for generations. Just about anything will work. A rare Blue Nile diamond, a decoder ring, or a piece of string will do the trick. It doesn't really matter where a ring comes from, as long as it means something special to the one wearing it.

We've been married now for more than thirty years. They haven't all been easy ones and they haven't all been hard. They've probably been a lot like your years, whether you're married or not. When Bob and I got married, we didn't know everything, but we knew enough. You do, too. We knew enough to seek out people along the way who can shape the way we see ourselves, the way we see each other, and the way we see Jesus. What we saw in the jeweler left a lasting impression on us, and we seek out people who understand the power of love, perseverance, and resilience to help us find those things in ourselves and each other.

Like the jeweler, we've been hurt and healed, and we continue to invite God to chip away at our flaws, like cuts in a diamond, so we can reflect the power of His love in this world.

CHAPTER 8

Board of Directors

The New York Stock Exchange is located at 11 Wall Street. I've never been there, but I've seen a couple videos. Most of them show the opening bell sounding, followed by a lot of people in dark jackets waving their arms in the air holding pieces of paper. If things go badly, there are even more people waving their arms and shouting louder. It looked pretty intense. My guess is that no one can hear anyone else because they're all yelling, but it doesn't seem to stop them from trying. Once, I met a person who worked on the floor of the Exchange and I asked why people do business this way. It just seemed unnecessarily chaotic. His response was simple. "It's just the way it's done."

I'm no stockbroker, but I know what it's like to raise a family. Sometimes it feels like the floor of the New York Stock Exchange, minus the dark jackets—or sometimes any clothing, for that matter, when our kids were young. Instead of an opening bell I had a clock radio, set earlier than anyone should ever need to wake up. I know God created everything, but I've always suspected dark forces behind the hours of one through six in the morning. The time of day that truly tests us.

I always keep my clock radio across the room, forcing me to get out of bed to turn it off. This early morning routine served me well when our children were growing up because, unlike Bob, I'm someone who needs a lot of runway to wake up. Most mornings I wake up blurry-eyed feeling like Bill Murray in the movie *Groundhog Day*, certain I'm reliving the same day over and over while Sonny and Cher sing "I Got You Babe." Don't get me wrong; I was delighted to live this day after day for decades. After all, I had wholeheartedly signed up for it.

Each morning, I knew that soon after I got up, more alarms would begin going off in the kids' rooms and the exchange floor would open again with lots of little arms waving. Instead of trading pork belly futures—whatever those are—the loud voices I heard were about lost homework and lunch bags, permission slips, and mismatched socks. There was constant noise in our home. Wonderful, earplug-piercing, deafening noise. The kind of noise that makes heavy metal music sound like a sonnet by comparison.

When I was in the thick of raising our family, most of the distracting noise didn't come from the kids; however, *it came from everyone else.*

I listened to advice on the radio and watched rented videos on how to raise a family. I read books. I went to moms' groups and women's Bible studies. I tried to take it all in. I didn't want to miss any opportunity to get advice or a great tip on raising a family. I thought if I got more information, I'd have what I needed to make all the right moves.

We all do this. We want more input and tips and data. More information isn't bad; it can actually be quite good. Here was the problem: There was just so much of it. I felt like I was on the trading room floor. The many voices combined became loud, inaudible static to me. Late at night, after the market closed and the kids were in bed, I'd be the one cleaning up all the paper off the floor again knowing it wouldn't be long before the bell rang the next morning and the noise would begin again.

People have always had a lot of opinions about marriage, parenting, and life. They have opinions about what to feed babies, what elementary school, high school, or college to attend, who to date, when to get married, where to live. There were conflicting ideas on working inside or outside the home, giving time-outs or corporal punishment. I met a couple people who had opinions about how much the tooth fairy should pay for a molar, whether I should be recycling, using fossil fuels or banana peels, you name it. If opinions came wrapped in hundred-dollar bills, I would've been a bazillionaire.

The more access I had to information, the louder the noise in my life got—and we had plenty of access. The decibels increased with every year. Eventually the sound became deafening to me. Everybody had advice in their hands waving it at me, and I couldn't take it.

I knew something needed to change, so here's what I did. I stopped listening to the loudest voices in my life and started listening to the truest ones. To do this, I needed to put together some trusted advisors. I didn't pick famous people like Mother Teresa or Colin Powell. I didn't look to a whole bunch of experts on the radio or around town who didn't know me; I decided to pick a couple people who were already in my life who did. They weren't the people who were up front leading the charge; they were the ones who were behind the scenes and had my back. I surrounded myself with a few people who made me hungry in my faith, strong in my resolve, and more available to my family. They were the ones who had the ability to touch my heart and nourish my soul. I thought of these people as my personal and private "board of directors."

I didn't make a big deal about it when I chose them. There were no announcements or confirmation hearings.

Most of them didn't even know they had the job. You've probably already picked yours; you just didn't realize you had. I picked a few people to listen to on purpose rather than listening to many people by accident.

Our meetings didn't happen in boardrooms with leather chairs, dim lighting, and crisply folded *Wall Street Journals*. They took place in school parking lots and living rooms and occasionally at coffee shops, if one of us had enough cash for a latte. They occurred on phone calls, over backyard fences, and outside of the library. These people didn't have a script or a speech, and they weren't trying to teach me anything; they were just accessible to me—and this taught me everything. Availability is the best teacher, and love is the only lesson plan we need.

One of the voices I valued as a young mother was my sister Cheri. We stood by each other's side throughout our childhood and then bravely set out to start families of our own. I called her whenever I needed motherly advice. She had a couple years on me and more kids than I did. She had earned her street credentials by being a wife and mother of five. If anyone had seen it all, it was her.

The day the principal's office called me because one of my kids had been snapping rubber bands with his seatmate, I had no clue what to do. I'd been sent to the principal's office as a kid in school; now I was an adult and was getting sent there again. I felt totally unprepared for this, so

I called Cheri. The best advice is usually the simplest, and hers was priceless. She told me to make sure my kid was okay, take the hit alongside him, enforce the consequences, and then go out for ice cream—not to celebrate the offense, but to diffuse things and to let him know I loved him.

We never ended up in the principal's office again. I don't think it was the ice cream; it was the wisdom of a seasoned mother of five who knew the immense and enduring value of restoring love and respect. Cheri's steady voice pointed me toward being the mother I wanted to be, instead of the upset and overreactive parent I thought I was supposed to be. She helped remind me I could be the kind of mom who could be tough on crime, but even quicker to reach for love. She called out of me the mom who was willing to sit patiently, if necessary, but would be even faster to stand with one of my kids no matter what. In countless ways, this has helped me as we've navigated other difficulties. When problems come our way, the kids know we don't need to wonder whose side we're on, because we've already picked theirs.

Leslie is another friend on my board. She's not famous for anything other than love, which makes her famous for everything in my book. We met in the back row of an aerobics class at church. Both of us were very pregnant and we needed to take breaks at the same time. We looked like a couple balloons with legs and I liked her right away. In many ways, Leslie is everything I'm not. She's an outgoing, blue-eyed blonde who makes gourmet food, speaks French as a second language, and has endless energy. What she accomplishes in one day, takes me weeks.

We taught our kids not to get into a car with anyone who didn't know the family password. Leslie was one of the few people who has it. She's thoughtful and was always available to come over. Whenever she needed to discipline her kids in front of mine, she would speak in French. To this day whenever my kids hear French, they wonder if they're in trouble. Leslie is the friend who will come over an hour before a party just to clean a toilet or take out the trash or chop onions.

She's come to our house in the middle of the night more than once. One time, I was in labor with our third child. If it weren't for her telling me it was time to get into the car with Bob, I'm sure we would've had a home birth. If we kept score of all the times she's bailed me out, she'd win by a big margin but she's the kind of friend who doesn't keep count. She just loves the people around her well and I'm one of them.

Finally, Chuck and Laurie live next door to us. Most of us don't get to pick our neighbors; they just come with the property line. If I could have picked mine, I'd pick ours. They're not just neighbors; they're like family. Laurie has seen it all. She's a wife, mother, grandmother, sister, aunt, and good friend to many. She is wise and kind, enthusiastic and sincere. We could have spent hours talking over a fence, but we decided instead not to have one between our homes at all. There's nothing separating where their property starts and ours ends. It's a lot that way with our lives, too. We just decided we'd do them together.

The day our daughter asked Chuck and Laurie to be her ring bearer and flower girl in her wedding, Laurie was so excited she ran over to our house while she was still on the phone with Lindsey just to celebrate the good news with me. Sometimes I think God gave us Chuck and Laurie to show us why Jesus said that how we loved our neighbor would reflect how we loved God. They love us that well. Most of the time I don't think Laurie even realizes the impact her words have had on me. Humble people are like that.

These are just a few of the people who have been on my board over the years. They aren't the only people who have influenced me, but they've stood at the front of the line during all of the important parts of my life. There have been many people who I've crossed paths with just when I needed them most. They're the ones who have been willing to stand back-to-back with me in whatever space I'm in—happy, sad, confused, frustrated, scared, or lonely. Having a board eliminated much of the noise I'd been hearing. I picked kind and empathetic friends who weren't afraid to celebrate the good days with me or love me throu~~gh~~ the bad ones.

Some people have many deep friendships, and others like me are wired for just a couple. Figure out how many friends God wired you from the factory to have and then go find that number. Don't compare the number of friendships you can manage with how many someone else has. I'd blow a fuse if I tried to maintain as many friendships as Bob has. Surround yourself with the right number of people who make you hungry in your faith, strong in your resolve, and more available to your family. This is your board.

Over the years, I've noticed a common thread in the lives of people I identify with. They're big-hearted and humble. They know how to have fun while also growing in their faith. They would rather serve up love than dish out opinions. If you ask them what they think, they'll tell you what lights them up, gives them joy, and about what they're learning. They know what they believe, but they don't go around acting like they're right all the time. When they have to choose between being right and being humble, they pick both because they know each have their own undeniable strength. My friends are fun, too. Some of them have serious jobs and serious things going on in their lives, but they all love to laugh. Paul talked about what makes a good friend. He described them as people who were completely humble, gentle, patient, and bearing with one another in love. Surround yourself with these people.

It's easy for me to fall into being unnecessarily serious. It comes from an honest desire to engage the world in a thoughtful and meaningful way. The problem is that serious had become my resting position. But Bob and these friends remind me that God also delights in our joy. They help me find my joy and they show me Jesus by what they do more than what they say—they say plenty with their lives. When they do speak, they don't use big words with me or with God. They know He isn't wowed by fancy words but delights in humble hearts. My friends are from different faith traditions and expressions. They live out their love in different ways, too. We don't vet the people we allow closest to us like they're applying for a job; we love them like we might be spending eternity together.

There's not a lot of trading done these days at 11 Wall Street. If you go to the New York Stock Exchange, there's only a few people on the floor. Computers do all of the communications now. The same thing is happening in many of our homes. Our kids have grown up and, honestly, I miss some of the chaos in the mornings. Not all of it—just some of it. I miss those distracting, arm-waving conversations that have been replaced with text messages with emojis and abbreviations that I don't always understand. Don't let technology replace all of the trading floor activity in your home. If you're at the front end of a family, prepare for it. If you're in the middle of it, press on. And if you're family is raised, like mine, be filled with gratefulness.

I am overjoyed there's no ticker tape at the bottom of the screen during the day measuring how each of us are doing in our lives. I can't lie. I think it would be great to be able to say love closed up 3/8ths on heavy trading around our house. But the truth is, we have all the information we need. We don't need to listen to the opinions of many. Find a couple people whose voices you trust. Listen to them. They'll let you know how you're doing. Ask God to help you navigate your way in the chaos. Sometimes our lives feel a lot like the stock market floor. The way God operates is really quite different. His plan from the beginning of time was that love wouldn't be traded among the noises in our lives; it would be understood in the places of peace. Sometimes when we're asking Him for an answer, He sends a friend.

CHAPTER 9

Running Away

When my children told me they were going to run away from home, I helped them pack.

When our kids were old enough to play in the backyard by themselves, it was as if their world opened up and our country's borders got a little bigger. Bob had given me a swing set for Mother's Day (best gift ever). It sat proudly on the little patch of grass in our small, private walled-in yard. Its wooden frame with two swings and a slide got a lot of use. It was usually me you'd find on it, but I'd let the kids have a turn every once in a while. It didn't take long before the grass developed skid marks under both swings. The marks looked like landing strips carved into the lawn. Where the grass died, the mud puddles grew and the slide was closed those occasional days, but the mud made the best body paint known to mankind. The gift that started as a swing set became many things. It changed and adapted, just as we did.

The swing set was my very own restful retreat while the kids took their afternoon naps inside the house. I would pine away the hours suspended from a few small chains and bolts. Something about gliding back and forth on a swing is still renewing for me. I let the distractions of the day fall away with every pump of my legs. The back and forth of the swing has mirrored much of the back and forth in my life. I always knew when I'd found my edge on the swing set when the corner legs lifted up off the ground as my outstretched legs reached for the sky and bounced back down again as I returned. It didn't feel as dangerous when I did it as it looked when the kids did the same thing. This was my life.

Our yard became a place where everyone was welcome. Carrots were grown, knees were scratched, mud pies were baked, and imaginations were set loose. We knew the neighbors by name on all three sides of our yard. It didn't take long before makeshift ladders were leaned up against the back wall so the kids next door could take the express route to join in the fun. From their early ages, leaving home, even if just to go to the backyard, became an important part of growing up. Independence wasn't a thing we feared for our kids; it was something we cultivated.

One afternoon, the kids took their newfound freedom a step further. They came running in from the backyard where they had been playing all morning and in unison announced, *"We're running away!!!!"* Their news wasn't a protest vote; it was a beautiful declaration of independence. The announcement was followed by many squeals of excitement and lots of jumping up and down. I wondered if this is how it was in Philadelphia for our founding fathers.

"Ohhhh, really?" I said, shooting them a smile while trying to match their sincerity. I told them I thought it was a fantastic idea, without admitting I'd wanted to do the same thing a few times myself.

We got right down to business, and I suggested they might want to bring some items when they go. Particularly, if they planned to be gone for a long time. I suggested they take two or three sandwiches, a few apples, and some licorice, you know, to get them through the first year or two. They'd want warm clothes if their travels took them from sunny San Diego to the snow country. They'd want to each have a flashlight so they could make shadow figures with their fingers against the tent walls at night. Yes, and a tent, too. One with several rooms. Maybe five or six. They could either make it out of pelts from buffaloes or bed sheets and coat hangers. I let them know I'd seen both and they seemed to work pretty well. The list was getting longer. They nodded their heads in wide-eyed agreement.

"This is going to be great!" I said. "Come on, I'll help you pack." The looks on their little faces were priceless. *You're helping us pack to run away? Is that even allowed?* I reassured them as they giggled that if we didn't move before they got back, we'd be right here. If we did leave, we'd put a map under the doormat so they'd know where to find us. Their spirits were daring, excited, and resolute. They were ready to face the unknown and to take on the world together. It was as if they had already discovered how much better adventures would be if they did them with each other.

Their running away was rooted in trust and confidence rather than escape or defiance. For most of us the same is true. We don't run away because we're filled with angst; we're wooed away by the promise hope whispers to us. Not only did they know they had each other's backs, but they also knew if it didn't work out, they would always be welcomed back home.

I admired their determination and grit. They were willing to give up their familiar spaces in order to experience a bigger world. In the best sense, we all need to "run away" every once in a while. When we run toward adventure, we end up learning more about the things that will last in our lives. Things like faith, love, trust, and belonging. These are things with staying power in our lives no matter where we go or how tough the going gets.

The packing was almost complete and each of their beds had a small pile of belongings on it. There's always a few last-minute additions to round out a move of this magnitude. A few comic books, a stuffed bear. Lindsey packed a journal so she could record all that happened on their travels. They picked up their piles, wrapped their treasures in bandanas, and tied them onto sticks to put over their shoulders.

I walked them to the door and told them I'd miss them terribly. Just before they headed out, I asked if they were going to take their hamster with them. They all looked at each other and then back at me blankly, as if they didn't remember they had one. That's the deal with running away. We move toward something that might look attractive, but we risk leaving a few important things behind by mistake. I went inside and grabbed the hamster, some food, and a handful of wood chips for their furry friend. There was no room in anyone's bandana for him, so he hitched a ride in someone's pocket.

I grew up seeing adventure and responsibility as two ideas in disagreement with each other; but I've come to realize they don't just coexist, they actually complement one another. For the kids, running away was actually launching out. Even if it was just outside the back door, leaving is what we all do at some point. Each of us leaves things every day, sometimes without knowing we are. It's the way we were designed by God. The trick is to leave the right things for the right reasons.

The kids started with nothing but their sticks and small bundles over their shoulders and each other at their side. It's what we all start out with, really. Our belongings might have a little more than a sandwich and a hamster in them. I've learned that all of the stuff I've accumulated in my life that doesn't fit usually isn't worth taking. Hopes and dreams pack easily.

The kids got to the back door, we said a prayer, I wished them well on their adventure, and then I went back inside the house, making sure they saw the back door shut behind me. I wasn't shutting them out or shutting myself in; I was helping them turn their next page. It's what we do for the people we love the most. It's what God does with us. They weren't really on their own, but they felt like it. Their journey didn't start in a distant land; it started in their own backyard. Our journeys usually do, too.

As I peeked through the bathroom window, I saw the kids all standing on top of a five-foot wall at the edge of the property line. In age order they climbed along the top of the wall at one end of the yard with their arms out like they were on a balance beam. This was more than just a trip to the other side of the yard. They were moving away from the safest thing they'd ever known without even realizing it. At some point we all need to do the same. Growing in our love means running toward opportunities to discover more of it.

From my vantage point, I could see their entire journey with the exception of a few seconds when they disappeared behind the garage. I know it was a few seconds because I was counting. "One one-hundred, two one-hundred, three . . ." I've always wondered if God does the same when we disappear for a while. He always knows where we are, of course, but it gives me a lot of comfort to think He still counts while He waits for me to return to Him.

For many of us, our journeys begin in our backyard, too. While Bob's travels often take him overseas and I'll join him from time to time, most of my biggest adventures happen near our home. Let yours start there, too. Figure out where God has planted you, how He has wired you, and then launch out from there.

God doesn't measure how high the walls are we scale; He sees our daring spirits. What would be a big deal for one of us might not be for someone else. God doesn't compare our leaps; He delights in them. The risk the kids took and the comfort they were ready to give up that day were huge to them. Life at home was good by most standards. They had shelter, a good school nearby, a few toys they liked, and parents who loved them. They hadn't complained about the service or the food, at least not to me. Sure, they had to make their beds, but overall their childhood experience had seemed tolerable. Yours probably was, too. The decision to run away wasn't anything personal; they simply had a great idea for something to do on an otherwise ordinary day. I'm learning to hope for a few incredible things for my ordinary days.

I always liked the stories in the Bible about the ones who ran away. A prodigal son, Jonah, Mary Magdalene, a guy named Peter. They all ran somewhere. I've wondered if maybe the one sheep in the parable wasn't lost at all; maybe it just ran away for awhile knowing it would return soon. When we do the same, God sometimes comes after us right away; and other times, I think He lets us return to Him a little later.

I've spent much of my life running away. There are a lot of reasons to run. Some people run away as a form of protest or a palace revolt and they vote with their feet. Others do it because they are ashamed of something that happened. Sheep aren't the only ones who get lost. More than a few shepherds do, too. When we do, God is infinitely loving and accepting of us. He knows we'll return changed and desiring the kind of comfort and security only He can provide to us.

We don't need to make our faith a lot more complicated than the kids did in their departure. They didn't have a plan; they had a bandana, a stick, a couple sandwiches, and a hamster. They just needed to climb the wall, get their balance, and go. Truth be told, with the exception of the hamster, that's all the rest of us need. We gather as much faith as we have and take it as far as we can. This is probably why Jesus told His friends to pack light.

The kids weren't gone for long. They walked around the outer edge of the property on the wall and were back home just in time for dinner. But here's the thing; they would have a story to talk about for years to come. Our dinner conversation that night had a different tone. It was filled with an air of excitement, a sense of accomplishment, and tremendous anticipation about where the kids might go next. Each experience is another chance to expand our borders. Every time, we print another invitation to show up and do the things we had only been musing about. When we finally get to the edges of our lives, we understand what is at the center of them.

Watching the kids on their adventure reminded me how much I still want the same in my life. These don't involve running away from problems, far from it. The best adventures involve leaving what's comfortable for a time. Long or short, it doesn't matter, only that we do it. The kids were running toward a beautiful adventure, not away from any difficulties. Don't be fooled. There's a big difference between the two. One's worth doing; one's worth staying and learning from.

The time it took for the kids to run away and return wasn't long. I don't think God keeps track of the time we're gone on our adventures either. Sometimes when we run, God multiplies our time to make it feel like we've been gone forever, but it's never very long to Him. Even if we do stay away for long, to Him it's like we just took a walk around the block. What feels like a long time for us must feel like a much shorter time to God who said a day is like a thousand years, and a thousand years is like a day. When we run away, I think He feels the same way I did about the kids leaving. He would certainly come find us if we didn't return; but He waits in constant anticipation of our arrival.

CHAPTER 10

A Neighbor's Love

grew up thinking a neighborhood had neatly arranged houses on tree-lined streets and friendly dogs licking the hands of happy mail carriers who were more likely to deliver valentines than bills. There were kids playing in sprinklers and station wagons in driveways. Everyone went back and forth borrowing cups of sugar, not because they needed them, but because they loved participating in acts of simple generosity. This wasn't what my neighborhood looked like growing up, of course, but this was the neighborhood I had made up in my mind.

Mr. Rogers's neighborhood was famous. Everyone wanted to be his neighbor. He invited young people into his neighborhood every week in his famous television show. People like me who didn't even like sweaters wanted to wear one just because Mr. Rogers did, and they wanted to be like him. His sweaters became both iconic and emblematic of goodness and kindness of being neighbors. What most people didn't know is that his mother made all of his sweaters. Who wouldn't love a guy who wore his mom's hand-knit sweaters every day?

He went into television for one simple reason: He didn't like what he saw on it. I think we each get to do the same in our neighborhoods. If you don't like what you see in yours, you have the opportunity to change it. It doesn't need to look like Mr. Rogers's neighborhood; in fact, it's better if it doesn't. His is already wonderful. Make yours look like yours. With or without the sweater, love looks great on everyone.

Neighborhoods come in all different shapes and sizes. I've never been to the International Space Station, but I've stayed in a Kibbutz community not far from the Dead Sea in Israel and have seen how the people there live in a collective community with one another. The Kibbutz is located near the lowest spot on the earth. The Space Station is located at the highest point above it. Each of these neighborhoods is different, yet like yours and mine they are defined by the people who live there, not the location or the structures. The Kibbutz isn't filled with people who are identical, the Space Station isn't filled with astronauts who are the same, and your neighborhood isn't either.

We all want the same things in life—love, purpose, and connection. It's that simple and that hard at the same time.

When a lawyer asked Jesus what the greatest commandment was, Jesus told him it was to love God with all of his heart and soul and mind and to love his neighbors. This means the ones living just outside our doors and the ones inside our homes, too. The ones at the bottom of the earth and the ones orbiting it and everyone in between. Loving our neighbors means loving everyone. Instead of getting stuck figuring out who and where my neighbors really are, I decided to just love the people who live the closest to me.

This isn't always easy. The hometown crowd can be tough. Jesus' neighbors probably thought He was better at making wooden picture frames than making bread and fish out of nothing. This isn't a reason to *not* start with the ones who don't think we're anything special. It's probably why Jesus said *to* start with these people. The Bible says a prophet is not without honor except in his own neighborhood, with his own relatives, and in his own household. I'm no prophet, but I know what it feels like to be misunderstood by the people I'm always around. You do, too. I think the reason for this is simple. They know all about our little peccadilloes, our faults, or our typicalness. It's the very reason Jesus said to start there, because it's the place where we could practice keeping it real.

I get amazed pretty easily. I think an oatmeal cookie is amazing. Bob picked some flowers for me and I thought they were amazing, too. I got stuck in a line trying to get a new driver's license, and I was amazed at how long it took. Yet, the Bible says there are only two times where Jesus was amazed. One happened in His neighborhood. He had returned to His hometown to preach in the synagogue and He was met with more than a little resistance. I can hear them saying,

"Wait, isn't that Mary and Joe's kid?"

"That guy? Isn't He just a carpenter?"

"What's *He* doing preaching in the synagogue?"

I bet Jesus wasn't surprised by this, but He did say He was amazed by it. Jesus said He was amazed by how little His neighbors believed. It's hard for all of us to see the familiar as holy. That's probably why Jesus decided He'd start everything He would eventually do in the world right in His own neighborhood where He was most familiar. He didn't start with a speech or a Bible study; He started with a party.

The only other time Jesus said He was amazed was when a soldier said all Jesus needed to do was say the word and his servant would be healed. Jesus was amazed at the soldier's belief. I want to be a little more like the soldier in my neighborhood. I want to believe that if Jesus just said the word, incredible, inexplicable things would happen in the lives of the people who live near me. And you know what? He said the word. He said if we'd love our neighbors, it was one of the most important things we could do with Him.

Sure, Jesus' neighbors were people who knew Him well; but just as important, Jesus knew them well, too. I imagine He could spot the nutty neighbors down the path. He could have questioned their character or the work they did, but this wasn't how Jesus lived. Much like He did with Peter, I bet Jesus saw the holiness in the ones around Him rather than their shortcomings. He saw things in them that they perhaps didn't even see in themselves. He wanted His neighbors to be amazed by God's greatness and He used His familiarity among them to do it. We can, too. We can't be well known by everybody, but we can be more fully known by our neighbors. Practice keeping it real where you live and you'll make Jesus real in people's lives.

Our neighbors aren't our projects and we're not theirs. I've learned most of what I know about loving my neighbors by being on the receiving end of the kind of love Jesus talked about from them. When I was in elementary school, a neighbor invited me to go to church with them for the first time. I felt included and it made me feel loved. In college, when my friend in the next dorm room asked me to join her for the weekend to visit family, I felt invited and it made me feel loved. I rented a guesthouse during college, and the owners of the main home welcomed me over for dinner and it made me feel loved. And when we moved into our house and the neighborhood women gathered for a tea party, I felt celebrated and it made me feel loved. Invite, include, welcome, and celebrate the people around you, and you'll be doing exactly what Jesus was talking about.

There are thirty-seven houses in our two-block neighborhood. I could tell you who lives in every one. We don't pick our neighbors, we just get them. I think God made it that way on purpose so we wouldn't get to choose. No one really moves out of our neighborhood; they just change the house they live in or go to heaven. We've moved three times on the same block. I'm not kidding. We're not the only ones either. More than a dozen of our neighbors have done the same thing. It's bizarre, but I think I understand why. The people here love their neighborhood, so nobody really wants to leave. It's the next-to-last resting place for a lot of neighbors here. Lord willing, it will be mine, too.

The people who live near us are interesting folks. I bet yours are, too. Go meet them. One of our neighbors evidently invented the colored ink for ballpoint pens. Another was a Navy Admiral who commanded the Pacific Fleet during one of our biggest wars. A famous R&B singer who sold more than one hundred million albums called our neighborhood home until he passed away. Because I knew the people who were my neighbors, I started liking ballpoint pens (with green ink), Navy ships, and rhythm and blues. You'll be the same way. You'll like the things that interest your neighbors, if your neighbors interest you enough to love them. Go ahead and risk it, then stand back and watch what happens to your heart.

Shortly after we moved into our house, one of our neighbors became bedridden and was under hospice care in her home. We hadn't known her for long, but it didn't matter. I was in my thirties and she was in her eighties. On paper we had very little in common, but as neighbors we had almost everything. I cut some roses from my yard, stuck them in one of my favorite vases, and wrote her a note. I thought this would be a quick drop-off, but when I knocked on her door, I was invited inside and into Wilma's room. I put the vase and flowers down on the nightstand next to her bed. I felt completely out of my depth. What would I say? Should I ask how she was feeling? Should I tell her how I was feeling? I wondered for a moment if I'd made a big mistake by visiting. Then Wilma's eyes met mine and I knew I hadn't. She reached out a weak hand and we held each other tightly. We weren't strangers, we were neighbors.

I leaned in closer. "Wilma? It's Maria, your neighbor from across the street." The corners of her mouth turned up just a little into a tender smile. I felt undeserving of her recognition, like a trespasser on holy ground next to her bed. I took a deep breath and whispered to her that we loved her. That's all I could get out before a speech-stopping lump welled up in my throat. She was dying in the neighborhood and I would go on living there. She was saying goodbye to her family and I was just beginning to raise mine. I think God wanted us to love our neighbors so we could learn how to bookend our lives from them.

We can't love our neighbors if we don't know them.

Wilma passed away a week later. Her home went up for sale along with everything in it. As we passed by the yard sale, our son Richard, noticed that the vase I'd brought over a few days earlier was for sale. Richard has always been wonderfully sentimental. Whenever we traded in one used minivan for another, he was the one in the family who felt sad for days. We knew we'd need to buy back our vase, a sweet reminder that loving our neighbor will cost us all of our love—and $1.75.

Zaida lived across the street from us. She had for years. She was five foot nothing on a stepladder. Years ago, our son Adam decided to set up a lemonade stand at the end of our driveway. Zaida was one of his first customers. Unbeknownst to us, Adam's handmade sign advertised fresh lemonade for five dollars a cup. That's a lot of money for a small cup of lemonade. Even more costly when you consider that more than a few of the lemons had come from Zaida's tree. Zaida got such a kick out of the kid's entrepreneurial ambitions. She already knew what we were only beginning to learn—that loving your neighbor is costly. I think she bought a half dozen cups that day. It's hard to imagine she actually drank it all.

Zaida had been widowed decades earlier. As she aged and considered the options available to her, we all agreed to put a monitor to transmit sounds in her house and the receiver in ours. We listened to Zaida for a year knowing if she had a problem, all she needed to do was call our names and we'd come running. It was a beautiful and practical expression of how neighbors can love each other where they are with what they need.

One evening, Zaida's daughter couldn't reach her by phone and called to see if we'd look in on her. We hadn't heard anything unusual, yet deep down I sensed something was wrong. Bob grabbed a flashlight and we went across the street to check in on our friend. We could see her unresponsive on the living room floor where she had succumbed to a massive stroke. Bob broke the window on her front door with the end of his flashlight and held her while we waited for the ambulance to come. That was the last time we ever saw Zaida in the neighborhood, yet she still remains a big part of it. Loving your neighbor makes it feel like they're still here even when they aren't.

One day another neighbor called and asked if I could help her pick out new flooring and paint colors for a remodel. She had lived in the house for years, raised her kids there, and decided it was time for a fresh look. She gave me a tour of her house and we walked past a cedar sauna standing in the garage. "You have a sauna?" I said. "That's amazing. Do you ever use it?" She laughed and patted my hand. "That thing stopped working a decade ago." She opened up the door so I could look in. Inside, on the bench was a little pile of books, a Bible, journal, and a list of every neighbor on the block. The sauna was her prayer closet. She leaned in and with a soft and sincere voice said, "You know, I pray for everyone in the neighborhood, especially the kids." With a twinkle in her eye, she added, "Yours in particular. I've seen how they ride their bikes up and down the street."

All of us have either come from a neighborhood or we live in one. It doesn't really matter how you define a neighborhood, as long as we recognize that we're a part of one. Stop waiting for a plan, or the annual barbecue, or a homeowners' association meeting. Just go love people. Start next door. Do it across the street. If the most important thing to God is our faith expressed in love, caring for our neighbors is one of the easiest ways to do it. You don't need to call it a "missions trip" because it isn't one. It's just a walk around the block.

CHAPTER 11

Work It Out

I love my life but it hasn't always been easy. When I was out of rehab and trying to rebuild new foundations for my life, I felt isolated even though I was surrounded by people at work all day. I suppose we've all felt that way at some point. I just didn't feel like I fit in anywhere. I wasn't the type to go out to parties with people I barely knew and I didn't want to stay at home every night either. More than anything, I craved a community of fun, wholesome people who were trying to figure out how to live out their lives and their faith in a genuine, engaged manner.

I knew enough about Young Life to know I liked the people in it. I had called Young Life's main office to see if they needed any volunteers and, surprisingly, they said they did. They told me they were going to take kids to a camp in Canada called Malibu that summer and needed a couple female leaders to get to know the high school girls who would be going. It sounded like fun, so I told them I was in. I don't think God maps out all of our destinations like it's a highway. I think He gives us a direction, like it's a path. Our part isn't to figure out all of the steps, just to take the next one. I had just taken mine.

Young Life usually meets in people's homes. They sent me to where Bob was leading because there weren't enough leaders for the girls, and they thought I could help out. I went to the address they gave me and walked into a room full of high school kids with a couple leaders in front. All of my insecurities from when I was in high school came flooding back. Was I wearing the right stuff? Who would I meet? Where would I sit?

None of us fully grow out of all of our insecurities; we just learn how to manage them. Sometimes we do this by disguising them with titles or careers or activities; and while we rarely fool anyone else for long, we can fool ourselves for a short time.

Apparently, from what I learned later, I had caught Bob's eye when I walked in. I was there to meet the high school girls sitting together on the carpet, not the guy up front who was in law school by day and volunteering by night. Don't get me wrong, I thought Bob was a nice guy and all. He seemed kind of fun, full of energy, and bounced around like a character from a Disney movie. When I met him, there were no fireworks going off, no doves flying out from behind his back as he reached out his hand and said hello to me. I learned much later that to Bob, since we had just said hello to each other, this meant we were dating. Guys are funny that way. I still don't get it.

As I slipped out through the back door after the Young Life meeting ended that night, Bob evidently turned to his friend Doug and said, "That's Mrs. Goff. I'm going to marry her someday." It took some rocky starts and stops, but we eventually went out on a few of the dates I told you about. They were no ordinary dates and Bob was no ordinary guy; yet on the very first night we met, I didn't see what Bob saw. I just wasn't looking for it.

I give him credit for being patient, because in the beginning we weren't operating on the same timetable. Bob has no gears. His resting position is full steam ahead. I had two gears at that time when it came to relationships, neutral and stop. I think God uses both styles. In order to merge our different timetables, one of the first things I needed to do before I got to know Bob further was to break up with him. I'm not kidding. The guy had it bad.

For a lot of us, we don't realize that what's right in front of us is what we've really been looking for. For many of us, we're just insecure enough or cautious enough or have been wounded deeply enough to think we don't deserve to find love. I think God understands this and so what He sometimes does is to send love to find us. As a little girl, I imagined love would come riding up on a stallion; but I've come to learn that it sometimes comes bouncing through the door at a Young Life meeting looking like Tigger.

From the minute we met, there was something different about the way Bob paid attention to me. He wasn't trying to dazzle me—he was trying to get to know me. It was a time in my life when I was focusing on other things I desperately needed, like growing in my faith, meeting new friends, and finding ways to help others. After a few bad experiences, I had sworn off dating and relationships completely. It always seems like it's during these times when we get blindsided by what we thought we wanted the least but actually needed the most.

Bob started leaving peanut butter and jelly sandwiches with notes under my car's windshield wipers. To this day, I'm not really sure why he did it. Perhaps he knew I would always need lunch and thought PB&J was a safe bet. Maybe he just figured it would work out better than leaving sushi or cheesecake. I have a feeling he simply wanted to give me something and that was what he happened to have. Either way, his thoughtfulness was touching and I took note, but I was still tremendously reserved in direct proportion to his enthusiasm in trying to get to know me.

Soon after we met, Valentine's Day was coming up. This is a holiday usually reserved for people already in relationships. When Bob showed up in the lobby of the advertising agency where I worked with a giant valentine card that was larger than him, I knew he had leap-frogged right past the friend stage and was in full pursuit mode. Call it intuition, call it a sixth sense, the gift of discernment, or whatever else it might have been . . . but I knew I'd either need to marry Bob or get a restraining order. Sure, I liked Bob a lot, but I knew I couldn't be in a relationship yet. I just wasn't ready.

A short time later, Bob showed up at my house with some furry cloth, a bag of stuffing, a couple buttons, and a needle and thread. He said he picked up all of the materials at the fabric store so we could make a stuffed bear together. "Oh my goodness," I remember involuntarily saying out loud. "You want to make a bear with me?" I knew I was in trouble. Everything he was doing to get my attention was so sweet, but so out of sync with my head and heart. I wasn't sure what to do. As he cut out the front and back outline of a bear, I sat next to him quietly freaking out. *Should I fake an asthma attack? Maybe I could create a distraction by lighting something on fire? Perhaps I'll light myself on fire.* All of the options seemed strangely viable in that moment.

Bob stitched a heart together for our bear and somehow he talked me into putting locks of each of our hair in it. As we sewed the fabric heart into the bear, I quietly panicked. *Oh my goodness, did we just make a child together?* I felt like Mary.

While I liked being on his radar, I needed to divert Bob's quiver full of love arrows that were all aimed directly at me. At the end of the evening, I made a sincere, but pathetic attempt to do the only thing I knew how to do, which was to sit him down and define the relationship. The dreaded DTR talk. It was a pretty short talk actually. It went like this. "You know how it looks like we're in a relationship right now? Well, we're really not in one."

Although I wanted to be kind, I resisted softening the message. I figured the chances were about one in a million that Bob and I would be a "thing." I knew if I even gave him that flicker of hope, he'd walk away saying, "So you're saying there's a chance!"

That night I watched as Bob walked out my front door and down the sidewalk with his head hung a little low and holding our stuffed bear by the arm. This was the second time I broke up with a guy I hadn't even gone out on a date with. Bob took it hard and clearly was disappointed, but he's a guy who knows how to love people well. Instead of acting like I'd just taken his lunch money, he treated me with kindness and respect and gave me the distance he knew I needed. This spoke the loudest to me about his character. He wasn't the kind of guy who brought a bunch of drama into his relationships. He knew that what made good plots for daytime television shows wouldn't make for a great life. Slowly my heart started turning toward his. I was experiencing firsthand a different kind of love. It reminded me of the way God pursues each of us. Creatively, hopefully, and relentlessly.

―――――

Eventually, Bob and I started dating. And if you haven't picked up on Bob's style already, it wasn't long before he took a knee and asked if I wanted to spend the rest of my life getting into mischief together. I wasn't sure then, and quite honestly still don't know all that I was agreeing to when I said "yes." None of us really do. It's the same when we say "yes" to Jesus. Much of what He invites us to happens off the map. Yet still, we come to trust in God's presence along the way and His promise that He doesn't come to bring drama into our lives but to fill them with purpose.

Bob continues to remind me that it's not a business trip God has invited us on but an adventure. The lessons we both learned through the period of our courtship continue to define our relationship even decades later. I don't keep breaking up with him now that we're married, but we're constantly having the DTR talk and redefining our relationship. Bob's not trying to tone down who he is to be me, and I'm not trying to ramp up who I am to be him. We're trying to be a couple of people who help each other be the fullest expression of who God is turning each of us into. We're not trying to keep things the way they were.

We want to be new creations and we know we can't be new creations if everything remains the same.

It's been a while since we made that teddy bear, but we got married and made a few people and it was both a lot more fun and a lot more expensive. We're still figuring the details out, but we're continuing to find new ways to pursue each other in love and express the bright light of hope, which shines in selfless acts of love, hope, and acceptance. Do Bob and I always nail it in the way we treat each other? No. But when we stumble along the way, we dust each other off and keep trying, confident that we'll get it a little more right the next time.

More than once, when Bob has walked in through the front door and our first interaction doesn't feel like the kindness and compassion we're shooting for in our relationship, I've sent him right back outside. I make him get back in the car and we take it from the top again. I'm not kidding. Good love sometimes takes some do-overs. In fact, it insists on them. Don't miss out on the chance to use a couple of your own. Each time you do, it's like putting a flag in the sand declaring what kind of love you want to inhabit your home. Raise that flag every day. It's a flag representing both surrender and resolve. Do whatever it takes to keep it flying high. Do something shocking. Do something tender. Do things that will constantly remind the people you love about what they mean to you. Don't shrink back when honest words of correction are needed, but find a way to express those words laced with love and grace. Remind yourself constantly that every act of extravagant grace is a declaration of immense love.

———

When I was home with three small kids, it didn't take long for life to overwhelm me. It didn't look like it was going to change any time soon and I knew something would need to change or I was going to lose it. I couldn't find the words to explain to Bob what I needed and I began to feel incredibly isolated and lonely. My head told me I should just tough it out, but deep inside my heart I knew I needed help. I knew I had an ally in Bob, but I just didn't know how to connect with him and let him know that behind my smile I was dying in a pile.

Bob's a guy who is in perpetual motion and, for as long as we've been married, he is constantly bouncing from one project and the next creative idea. I love that about him, but all of this left me feeling even more isolated and alone. One afternoon while I was in a store with the kids, I saw a display of storefront signs. One of them said in large black letters "Help Wanted." In a moment of personal honesty and clarity, I thought to myself, *Boy, isn't that the truth*. I knew I needed help but hadn't found the words until then. I bought the sign and put it in the front window of our home that afternoon. Then I waited for Bob to return at the end of the day. The sign was a simple, honest declaration. This was my flare, not shot at Bob, but high into the air above him asking for help.

If we're to continue to grow into the people God wants us to be, we need to constantly be looking for new and better ways to let the people we love know where we're at and what we need. Do it often. If you've been quietly sucking it up, stop it. Start communicating your needs. It's only in vulnerability and with this kind of transparency that our deepest needs become visible to the ones God has given us to bear them with us.

Will you be misunderstood if you start communicating your needs to the ones you love the most? You bet you will. When Bob saw the sign, he didn't think I was asking for help, he thought I meant he needed help. He was both right and wrong. Have the conversation anyway. Push through the awkward middle part, because you'll get to the other side of it feeling more loved and understood.

While that sign sat in the front window until Bob got home, I imagined some random person seeing the sign and coming up to the front door to ask about the job. It made me realize that communicating our needs requires understanding them. Instead of just feeling generally overwhelmed, I had to figure out what I actually needed help with. When I put my sign up, I wasn't sure what I really needed. So before Bob got home, I took the time to figure out as much about my specific needs as I could. Don't expect that you'll figure them all out in one sitting. It will probably take a couple honest times of soul-searching. But the treasure is always worth the search.

I forced myself to be honest and practical. I didn't have or want any canned answers. Honestly, what I wanted at the time wasn't an exotic vacation or new car, and while world peace would be amazing, what I really needed was a babysitter a couple hours one day a week while I ran errands. Most of us don't need a lot; we just need a little of the right things. Figure it out. Start your list. Do it for yourself. Do it for your family and friends. Get your "Help Wanted" sign out, figure out what your job description is, what you need, and stop keeping it a secret. I know it's tough, but don't wait any longer. Letting the ones around you know your needs now is a lot better than ignoring them and having the weight of them result in needing an "Out of Business" sign hung in the window.

Your friends and spouse can't fix your problems or mine, but they can help guide us back to ourselves and our Creator. Don't just be on the receiving end. Make it your life's work to ask people what their needs are. Ask them how you can help them become the person God wants them to be. Don't give any suggestions. Some of the best advice I've ever received when I was overwhelmed was a hug. Give plenty of those. They're always good medicine. The journey of asking, learning, growing, mending, stretching, and discovering is what heals our pain.

Sometimes the help we need, we can get from a friend, and other times we might figure out we need a good counselor. I've taken advantage of both. I'm like a carrot. I stay in one place and grow deep and long. I live most of my life under the surface. Bob jokes that seeing me in a crowd is like seeing a unicorn. Bob, on the other hand, is like a guy shot out of a cannon. Every morning he climbs in, points toward the biggest collection of people he can find, reaches back, and lights the fuse. Shoot a carrot out of a cannon and you have bad salad. Plant a cannonball and you'll go hungry. Whether you're married or single, figure out what fuels your passions and what crushes your soul. Figure out what you're good at and what you're not so good at. Keep it simple. Do more of what you're good at and less of everything else.

Because we're so different, Bob and I have invited trusted counselors who are good at what they do to coach us. I'll admit, Bob was a little hesitant to go to counseling at first, but we've seen beautiful things emerge by doing the heavy lifting together. We've been figuring out what we each need and, even more importantly, how to express it. I've learned a great deal from the time we've invested about forgiveness, grace, patience, and speaking the truth with love. I've also learned that when I'm feeling the most weighed down, it's not Bob who is the enemy; it's often the enemy flaunting my past that's been doing the talking. Understanding where we've been can help each of us navigate where we're heading. Do your work.

We're both learning new and more generous ways to see our differences as our strengths. I found a picture of Bob taken when he was about eight years old. In it, there's a freckled-faced, redheaded little boy leaning up against a big tree trunk reading *Dr. Doolittle*. It's a stolen moment captured in this timeless photograph. It was taken in a rare couple minutes when Bob wasn't getting into mischief or playing with fireworks and blowing his eyebrows off as he's prone to do. The photograph also frames a moment of calm and wonder and innocence. When Bob hasn't interacted with me the way I wished he had and I want to make him the enemy, I get this small picture out and look at it. It reminds me that there's been nothing sinister about him then or now. He's just a big version of that little kid leaning up against the tree who simply messed up. Doing this lets me be not only a little more generous in my thoughts but a lot more accurate, too.

Find a photo of yourself when you were eight. Do it now. Go frame it and talk to that person. Let that younger version of you know you still see them. You know who they are and what they went through and what happened next. Tell that younger version of you that you know about the celebrations and the pain they've experienced. Then ask them about what they need to get to where God is taking them next, now that they've grown up and turned into you. Do the same thing for the people you love. Find photos of them when they were kids. Ask them what they want. Talk to them about who they are. It might take a while for them to find the words, but be patient. You'll find the right words to work it out together.

CHAPTER 12

I'll Be Back

It's common for junior high schools to send their eighth grade students on a field trip to Washington, D.C., to understand more about how our government operates. These students fly in from all over the country, visit historical monuments, learn about the history of our country, and sometimes meet with elected officials. It's an amazing experience for them.

During the spring of 2001, our daughter's trip was planned to happen the following school term in November. What none of us had anticipated during the planning was the terrorist attacks on September 11, which occurred shortly before everyone had been scheduled to leave on the trip. As the date approached for Lindsey to leave, deep down I really didn't want her to go. Other possible attacks and her safety were swirling in my mind. A trip to the capitol, which once sounded great, now sounded risky.

That said, we also didn't want to give in to fear and cancel Lindsey's trip. If we did, it would feel a little like we let the bad guys win. We were conflicted about the idea of her going and also about her staying.

After talking it through with Bob at length, we arrived at the airport to drop Lindsey off, and we still felt unsettled as we saw sixty junior high school kids and a few well-meaning parents who would do their best to look after them. They all stood in a group by the ticket counter. Bob and another dad decided on the spot that the only way they would feel comfortable with their kids going is if they were nearby. Without telling anyone, they quietly booked tickets on another airline leaving later that day. Their plan was to keep a watchful eye on the kids without spoiling their adventure or letting them know they were there. If anything dangerous did happen, they would never be more than a stone's throw away.

When I returned to the airport for the second time that day, I thanked Bob for being the kind of dad whose love for his kids came first. As he got out of the car he said, "Everything's going to be okay; I'll be back." It reminded me of what he had told me years earlier while belaying me up a cliff rock I was climbing.

I imagined Bob and the other dad getting to Washington, D.C., putting on fake glasses with plastic noses, sitting on park benches, and looking at the kids through small holes poked in newspapers. Inside larger venues like the Smithsonian, I imagined the two dads with *Wall Street Journals* held high, talking to each other on walkie-talkies. None of this turned out to be necessary, of course; the kids were safe and they probably didn't need to hide. They just kept a close and ever-present watch on the young kids without taking away from their adventure. Seeing these fathers take steps to be present, available, near, and ready to provide protection reminded me of the way God watches over all of us. He doesn't wear costumes and go under-cover; He doesn't need to. He's everywhere. He doesn't need the fake nose and glasses either because He's not try-ing to hide from us.

The reason Bob and the other dad didn't let the kids know they were near was simple. They wanted to be pres-ent without interfering with the growth that would come as the kids experienced new things on an adventure. Good dads do that kind of thing. They let their kids practice their independence while remaining close at hand. God does the same. It's in His nature to be with us in everything, both the good and the bad. He doesn't elbow His way into our lives. Instead, He surrounds us with love. He's present in our lives the way Bob and the other dad were present in Lindsey's and her classmates' lives.

Without Lindsey even seeing Bob, she was always under the watchful eyes of a loving father who was present.

God doesn't keep a secret about His presence because He doesn't trust us; in fact, the opposite is true. He does it so we'll grow, secure in trust of the protection provided by His presence, even when we're not aware of it. He doesn't force Himself into our lives. He loves us and is content to be with us always whether we know He's there or not.

A few months after the trip, Bob came clean and told Lindsey he was there the whole time during her adventure. It's not unlike what God did with His kids throughout the Bible when He told them that He had been with them every step, even when they didn't realize it. When God told His people He had been with them, they weren't disappointed and they didn't feel like God was spying on them. It was the opposite. They felt protected. Lindsey did, too. When I look back at all of the times God was with me, even when I didn't realize it, I get a peek at the love of a Father for me even when I didn't know I needed Him.

The closest I've come to seeing what absolute dependence and devotion looks like is when we got our dog. We had him for fifteen years. His name was Riley, but Bob called him "ratdog." I'm not sure if it's a guy thing, but as soon as Riley came home to us, it was like Bob needed to establish himself as the alpha dog in the house. We went along with it and pretended Bob was the head honcho, but we all knew Riley ruled the place.

At the time we decided to get a dog, Bob seemed pretty set on having us get a big dog. I was doing the shopping though, so I got us a tiny toy poodle instead. That's just the way it goes. I explained to Bob when it comes to picking out the dog, you must be present to play.

Riley was a part of our family almost from the beginning. He had his own hashtag and more followers than most. He got his hair groomed more often than the rest of us combined, and it usually cost twice as much. His medical expenses were getting higher the older he got. He was blind in one eye and deaf in both ears. He had all four legs, but because of his arthritis, he walked like he only had three. The older he got, the more things he bumped into. I know how he felt. Yet, with all his ailments, his love and loyalty to me had never wavered. He didn't know what to do with himself when I was gone, he would sit and stare blankly into space and shiver until I returned. I made him employee of the month mostly because he was the only one at home after the kids left for college.

I got us a poodle because Bob has allergies and we had heard poodles were hypoallergenic. I thought that meant Riley wouldn't make Bob sneeze. But it turns out "hypoallergenic" apparently meant that Riley was allergic to people. There were really only a couple people Riley liked, and I think I was both of them. I got to be the master that fed him, cleaned him, held him, and took him to the vet.

Bob pretended he didn't like the dog much and teased about him all the time, but I heard him snuggling with Riley and saying ridiculously affectionate things to him at night before he tucked Riley under the covers with him, so I know it was all an act. Still, all the nice talk aside, Riley was entirely devoted to just me. Because he was completely devoted to me, if I got up, he got up. Where I sat, he sat. During the odd time when he was awake, he was like a dryer sheet stuck to my pant leg. As far as Riley was concerned, the sun rose and set on me. I kind of liked that. Who wouldn't.

He just didn't know what to do with himself when I wasn't in plain sight, so it was my practice for his entire life that when I left the house, I'd hold my hand up and say to him, "You stay; I'll be back." It's a simple idea, but a comforting one to him. At first, it took him a little while to get a sense of what I was saying. There's something comforting in familiar words and gestures. I think we all need this kind of assurance from the ones we love. It's the same kind of assurance we need from God when we can't see Him, too.

When you raise young kids and everything goes the way you hoped it would, you work yourself right out of a job. What I've come to realize is that as our kids grow up, we work ourselves right into another.

Our kids became adults and as they did, the business of raising them slowed considerably. While demands for our time and direction have decreased over time, I've made sure that customer service has improved. Bob and I are more available to travel together, spend time together, and develop areas of our life that have been wonderfully on hold for decades.

Lindsey was our first to leave for college. She picked Seattle Pacific University and our whole family came to help her move in. When the last box was unpacked, we went to lunch before saying our final good-byes. We ended up at the famous Public Market in downtown Seattle. Bob pulled up in front, put the car in park, and jumped out with the boys. A few minutes later, the guys were back at the car holding big bouquets of flowers for us.

With Lindsey being the first to leave, we all knew our family nucleus was changing. We huddled together outside the car. A mixture of excitement, uncertainty, joy, and heartache hung over us.

What do we do now? each of us wondered silently.

How do we say good-bye in moments like this?

Bob suggested we pray for Lindsey. Bob is a big softy and didn't get many words out before he got all choked up and gestured to our son Richard to continue. Richard didn't get much further before he couldn't talk and he turned to Adam to pick up where he had left off. Adam was only good for a word or two as well. For the first time in our family all five of us were speechless. Still, everyone's lump-in-the-throat silence spoke volumes to Lindsey. It didn't get easier sending the next two off to college when it was their turn. We knew that we were going to go home and stay, and they'd be back. One of the traditions we have that has helped us in these moments actually comes from watching the Navy ships where we live in San Diego.

There are three aircraft carriers stationed near us with dozens of fighter jets on the deck of each. Before each jet is launched from the catapult, the last signal the pilot gives the deck crew is to put their fists together with thumbs out and bounce them together. It's the signal to "pull the chocks." The chocks are what keep the wheels in place and keep the plane from moving.

Sending Richard to college wasn't any easier than sending Lindsey. After getting all of his things in his dorm room, we gathered in the middle of Richard's room and prayed for his upcoming year. Someone said "amen" and we all looked up. We knew it was time to go, but no one really knew how to leave. Bob slowly reached up with his hands, put his fists together with his thumbs out and bounced them. It was time for us to pull the chocks. We all lost it. It was time for Richard to launch. We'd stay back at home, and we knew he'd be back.

These days, the "pull the chocks" hand signal has become a universal signal for our family when it's time to move on. We use it often. I've seen Bob signal me from across the room at dinner parties and even once or twice at church if things were dragging a bit.

As each of the kids left for college, I learned a new appreciation for how good every stage of life can be from the time they landed to the day they launched. Every season has its trade-offs. With more freedom comes opportunities, life experiences, and growth for everyone. Every season hasn't just become better, they've only been different. Pulling the chocks isn't easy, but it's what God intended. It's about beautiful change in our lives and leaving and cleaving in marriage. He created people and families and gave us a relatively short period of time to be alive together. We love them, then we launch them, then we love them some more. Here's the thing. The ones we love can't come back if we don't let them go.

When Jesus said goodbye to His friends, they probably felt uncertain, lost, and uneasy. I bet they experienced many of the same emotions I did when I saw my kids leave and as Riley did when he saw me leave. Sensing this, Jesus told them before He went to be with His Father that He'd be leaving, but not for long. Jesus said He'd leave behind His Spirit and He would be a comforter, a counselor, and a guide we could trust. It's like He put His hands together, with thumbs out and said, "You stay; I'll be back."

CHAPTER 13

Fear Not

Cigarettes come with warning labels to let people know they will make you sick, or worse, will kill you. Fear doesn't. It wraps itself in careers and relationships and behaviors. Still, its effect can be just as lethal. Fear wags its bony finger at all of us from the shadows. It's a disease all of us catches at one time or another. We don't catch it because somebody coughed; we get it because we're easily distracted. We're all at risk of losing sight of the beautiful things that give us confidence and courage to be sure, but some of us are a little more at risk than others. If we look to the people around us to validate our values or feelings or faith, we're a soft target for fear. We all have questions and doubts. Don't ignore them; keep it real. Jesus never had a problem with the people who had a lot of questions. He was concerned with the ones who thought they had all the answers. Fear is a dead tree riddled with hopelessness, cynicism, and self-doubt. Be a sapling, reaching up with courage and bravery and faith. Fear gets a lot of attention— way more than it deserves. It's not surprising because fear is never content on the fringes; it always demands center stage.

Growing up, I remember walking home from elementary school when a bully named Derek jumped out from behind some bushes as I passed by and grabbed me. My books and lunch box skidded across the sidewalk. Without thinking, I kicked him hard. I guess the kick landed where it counts, because he collapsed long enough for me to collect my stuff and run away as fast as I could. That was the first time I can remember experiencing how fear triggers something deep within us. It helps us defend ourselves, but at the same time can debilitate us from helping anyone else. Fear helps us both find and lose our edge because it points us toward safety.

I've spent much of my life in fear. I've been as afraid of failing as I have been of succeeding. I've been afraid of being in trouble and being too good, being ignored and being recognized. Just like Derek, these were all just bullies jumping out from behind the bushes in my life.

Sometimes we try to control what we don't understand. I remember trying to survive my fears by controlling the things that made me afraid. I felt the need to control circumstances, outcomes, and people like they came with steering wheels. I thought if I could dodge making eye contact with a teacher or do everything perfectly, I could escape the people who made me feel vulnerable and insecure. Sadly, it didn't work; it never does. Fear delights in our attempts to avoid or ignore it. The antidote that gives us the buoyancy to rise above our fear is found in love and hope and the kind of peace we don't try to manufacture but experience in courageous gratitude.

Peace fills up from beneath love's reservoir, not above it. It's not a layer; it's the overflow, the surplus. It's not what's left over; it's the origin and it's most available and abundant where courage and faith flow the strongest. We find it as a little girl at a YMCA camp on Catalina Island or as a soldier in a firefight. When we're feeling vulnerable and afraid, we can't experience the supernatural peace that comes from God's brand of hope and love. Faith doesn't eliminate fears in my life; it lets me know I had someone I could bring them to.

As I got older and started my own family, the biggest lesson I learned is how completely irrational and uncontrollable my fears actually felt to me. Fear is both cunning and subtle. Like an inaudible dog whistle, it operates at a wavelength I feel only I can hear. It sends out a high pitch that can look like a career, or a relationship, or a tragedy. It will promise us water, then lead us down to the bottom of dark wells and drown us there.

As a young mother, I felt God nudging me to find a way to let go of fear after terrorists attacked America on 9/11. Most of us over twenty years old can remember exactly where we were and what we were doing when we heard the tragic news that day. Bob had just left for work and I was getting the kids ready to drive to school. I looked up and was surprised to see Bob come back through the front door. The look on his face was somber and I instantly knew something was wrong. He calmly and carefully explained what he had just heard on the radio. It was hard to comprehend what he was saying. Something about *buildings . . . civilians . . . airplanes.*

Just like that, in a matter of seconds, time seemed to freeze as the weight of this new reality hung in the air in our home. What were we supposed to do next? My first instinct was to take my little family and hide. If this attack meant we now needed to live the rest of our lives behind locked doors, safe from bad guys, I would have gladly made that sacrifice. Fear threatened to get the best of me.

That night during dinner, our family talked about the events of the day. We were sad and confused, and Bob and I tried to answer the questions the kids asked. We answered with quite a few "I don't knows" that evening. Eventually, the conversation turned to what this would mean for the future of our country and the world. We wondered what the leaders of other countries might be thinking that night as well and felt empathy for them as they needed to decide how they would lead.

Bob asked the kids, "If you could spend a few minutes with a world leader, what would you want to ask them?" They each had a different perspective. Adam was ten and wanted to invite them to come visit us in our home sometime. Richard was twelve and wanted to ask these leaders what they put their hope in, considering the bad things that just happened. Who knows? Maybe he was hoping for the same things. Lindsey, who was fourteen at the time wanted to know if she could go to their country to conduct a video interview with them.

As our conversation continued that night, one thing led to another and over the next few weeks the kids wrote letters to hundreds of leaders all over the world asking their questions. We dropped the letters in the mail and waited not knowing what would happen next, but assuming they would get a pile of polite *no's*.

The day after 9/11, Billy Graham spoke at the Washington National Cathedral in a televised service. At a time when our country was mourning the loss of so many lives, it was hard to know what to do next. His message reminded us, in the aftermath, we were faced with a choice: "Either to implode and disintegrate emotionally and spiritually as a people and a nation, or we might choose to become stronger through all of the struggle to rebuild on a solid foundation."

It turned out we weren't the only ones who wanted to become stronger through the struggle. We started to get responses to the kids' letters. There were plenty of no's as expected, but there were some yes's, too! Leaders from a host of countries responded with invitations for them to come to their country for a meeting. These included invitations from the President of Israel, the Prime Minister of Switzerland, the Vice President of Bulgaria, and many more. I knew I didn't want fear to call the shots for us.

We had to go.

As we packed our bags to travel overseas for the first time, the fears, questions, and concerns we had were replaced with anticipation about what might happen. Out of the depths of loss and confusion, an unexpected message of love and hope had sprouted. Fear couldn't keep it underground. It didn't work on Jesus and it wasn't going to work on us.

———

On the first of many trips to meet with the leaders who had extended invitations, we landed in London in the rain. There were news reports of still more attacks being anticipated. A terrorist group had shot a missile at a commercial airplane heading for Israel a day earlier. It was the same airline we were to fly into Israel in a few days. Another attack in Tel Aviv had targeted a crowded city bus that day and the lives of more innocent civilians had been lost in the neighborhood we would be staying in. This news fanned the embers of fear I thought I had snuffed out and my concern for the safety of my family was ignited once again. Fear is a lot that way. It finds safety in hiding just beneath the surface.

That night as we all settled into our hotel rooms, Bob and the kids fell fast asleep, but I was wide-awake. I could feel my jaw tighten as I clenched my teeth. The wave of fear passed through me from head to toe like an electric current. I tried my best to get away from the feeling. In the dark, I grabbed a pillow and my Bible and headed for the bathroom. With the door shut, I sat on the cold tile and started reading my favorite passage in Philippians. I read the words out loud over and over again. *Be anxious for nothing. Be anxious for nothing. Be anxious for nothing.* I said it again and again into the darkness. There's more to the verse, but these four words were as far as I could get.

The fear of rocket-launched missiles and exploding buses was real. The battle in my mind grew louder. I wanted to wake up my young family, pack up our bags, and head in the other direction. No doubt everyone would understand why. Thankfully, I also knew what I really needed was to change the narrative of my fearful thinking and replace it with being obedient to the small part I felt was ours to do as a family. Sharing love and hope requires courage and presence.

Even though I've felt justified in feeling afraid many times, I've been asking God to replace my absolute fear with total peace. Am I there yet? Nope. But I'm heading in that direction. I'm learning when I start to be afraid to simply breathe. I imagine I'm breathing in courage and exhaling fear.

A few hours later on the bathroom floor, I was able to believe wholeheartedly the rest of the message in that familiar passage in Philippians: But with everything, in prayer, give your requests to God and the peace of God will transcend all understanding, and it will guard your hearts and minds in Christ.

The next day on the flight, I began to pray for safety for us, for the flight and flight crew. Heck, I even prayed for laughter, fun, and making memories. I prayed for unfamiliar food, clean water, and rest along the way. These are things we all pray for at one time or another. Near or far, home or away, our basic needs rarely change. I don't think God ever tires of these prayers. I think He celebrates in their familiarity.

We landed in Tel Aviv. Security vehicles with flashing lights appeared on the tarmac. Their job was to escort the plane to the gate. Security was on high alert; because I'd been talking to God the whole trip, fear wasn't.

Inside the airport, the customs officer who held all of our passports looked perplexed when Bob explained our kids had been invited to meet with their President to tape a message of hope of love. "Isn't that terrific?" Bob asked. The two locked eyes for a second and he gave the nod to carry on. Every single request I made to God that night in London on the bathroom floor was replaced by His peace. If God is that faithful, I want to be, too.

The bully tries to scare us by hiding in the bushes or jumping out from behind them. Don't fall for it. Fear's goal is to keep us stuck in our tracks. Don't let it. Courage and bravery doesn't always look like someone leading the charge up a hill in a war; sometimes it looks like a couple kids demonstrating God's love in the world. I am grateful for the many people I've met who have shown me the undeniable power of kindness and love to beat fear back with a stick and, if necessary, to kick it right where it counts.

CHAPTER 14

Be Ready

I have a list of things I want to ask God when we meet face-to-face. I'm not sure if we'll all be standing together shouting our questions like we're at a press conference, or quietly raising our hands like we did in elementary school waiting to be called on. Honestly, I don't think either will happen. Instead, I think He'll pull each of us in close and let us ask Him about what we've been most curious about during our short lives. With a reassuring nod, He'll whisper His answers to us one at a time. I think most of us will understand for the first time what was obscured by our limited life experiences or small views of Him during our lives.

He won't be in a hurry when we ask Him our questions and He gives us His answers, and He'll be glad, for once, we aren't either. I'm not sure how long it will take, but I'm guessing just about forever, which would explain why He made eternity to last so long. I realize the things I wonder about the most right now might not matter that much to me when we get to heaven. Still, I put a high value on being ready, so I've written my questions down so I don't forget them.

You know what I'd want to know first? I'd ask God about my short thumbs. I know it sounds insignificant and silly, but I've always wondered if He made them a funny shape so I'd delight in His creativity, or so I wouldn't be able to beat everyone at thumb wars?

And why is it that I can write backwards in cursive (I really can), yet I struggle to write the simplest of words correctly?

And why do I get tongue-tied speaking to people, yet I'm one of the few people I know who can tie a cherry stem into a knot in my mouth? And honestly, why instead couldn't He let me sing like Natalie Grant? Or paint like Van Gogh?

And why do elephants have amazing memories, yet I can get to the grocery store and can't remember what I drove there to get?

I wonder how my quirks, oddities, and shortcomings contribute to God's enormous and beautiful plan for the world.

I'd also ask God how He decides who gets what, and why we spend so much time looking at what each other is doing, rather than just running our own race.

I was in a track race in high school. The track coach had us line up; we got our feet planted in the blocks and looked down the long track. He lifted his starting gun into the air and said, "Get ready . . . Get set . . . Go!" and fired the gun. I've spent way too much time on the "get ready" part. I do this by making lists. Heck, my lists have lists. It's ridiculous. Here's how I do it.

I keep my list of questions I have for God on Post-it notes in my Bible. I've probably got as many notes in there as there are Bible verses. Being ready is good, I suppose. It's the first thing the track coach wanted us to do. It's why we have fire drills in schools, and it's why I have a first-aid kit in the car. The Bible talks a lot about the virtues of being ready. There's even a story of ten women who took their oil lamps to greet the groom before a wedding. Five were ready and five weren't. The ones who weren't ready forgot to bring extra oil; the ones who were ready had more than enough. You remember how the story went. The groom finally arrived and the ones who were ready went to the party and the ones who weren't didn't get to go.

I'd hate to miss even a minute of a party Jesus threw because I wasn't ready. I think we all would. Here's the thing. He's not just talking about a party that happens in heaven; He's throwing the party right now and He wants all of us to come. Sure, there will be more celebrations to come in heaven, but the party is already happening. Right now, right here. I've wondered if some of us are so busy getting ready for the one in heaven that we're missing the one that's going on right now. Being ready is a good thing until it distracts us from being present. When eternity's starting gun sounds, I don't want to find I was so busy obsessing over getting ready that I forgot to show up at the race.

There's a big difference between getting ready and being willing. There's a lot more people who are ready than are willing. More often than I'd like to admit, I'm one of them. I think I know why. Getting ready is safe. Getting ready is something we can control. It gives us an excuse. It's been providing us cover for years. It's like we settle for just being *at* the race as long as it looks to everyone else like we're *in* the race. At some point I decided to stop spending all of my time just getting ready and work on the "get set" and "go" parts.

Getting "set" for me is making sure I've got firm footing. For a runner, it's planting their feet solidly in the blocks. For me it's planting myself firmly with Jesus. God wants us to know what He has to say. We won't know what He has to say about what He wants if we don't read what He said. The Bible is His voice on paper. Unfortunately,

some of us get stuck at the "get set" stage—always study-
ing the Bible but never getting out of the blocks and doing
what it says. Don't settle for having an opinion when you
can be an example.

Don't get me wrong. Getting our footing is important,
but as good as it is, there's a false safety in preparation. The
thing about preparation is you can always do more. Life in
the blocks is the only time in the race where I was tied with
everyone else for first. Sadly, I forgot it's the only time we
were all tied for last, too. I need to remind myself that getting "set" is what we only do in the short moments before
the gun sounds; it's not the place to camp out.

It used to concern me that Bob traveled to countries in
conflict zones where in some of these places he needed to
wear bulletproof vests. I stopped reading the lists of State
Department travel warnings a long time ago because they
caused me to freeze in fear. "Wait, what?" I'd ask myself as
I read the warnings. Bob reads the same warnings as warm
invitations to go. Honestly, at first, I just didn't get it. Why
go to Somalia, Iraq, and the Democratic Republic of the
Congo? Or to remote parts of India or Mongolia or Uganda?
The more we talked about it, the more sense it made though.
Some twenty-three of these places have tremendous suffering
and the opportunities there to make a difference are huge.

Bob wanted to use his legal training to help those in
need. One of his early trips overseas was to India, a place

the whole family has traveled to together. Bob met a man named Moses more than a dozen years ago. Moses is a good representation of his namesake in the Bible, and he does much of the same work. He helps set people free. Bob was starting a nonprofit human rights organization to fight for justice and freedom for widows, orphans, and children who couldn't speak for themselves. Doing this is both simple and hard. It's as simple as showing up. It's hard because it means we're apart.

Bob, Moses, and some others made plans to investigate a red-light district where little girls were being held in brothels against their wills. Tragically, many of these little girls had been sold to brothel owners by family members. These girls had no one to turn to for help. Fortunately, there are many wonderful organizations who find these young girls, rescue them, and help them develop the skills to earn an income and their freedom. We decided we'd be one of them.

In order to gather surveillance video in the brothels, Bob has cameras that look like pens and watches and he needs to wear clothes to help him blend in, which is tough for a six-foot-four light-skinned American. A few days before Bob's trip I picked Lindsey up from school and told her we needed to make a stop at Marshalls and get a shirt for her dad to wear into a brothel. It was one of the more unusual and yet funny conversations we've had.

I look forward to Bob's calls when he travels. I love hearing his voice and the stories from the day. It helps me to know how to pray for him when he's away and assures me he's okay. Even when we're far away, somehow we still feel very close.

Sometimes when I'm just waking up, he is going to bed wherever he is. He'll call and ask over a bad phone connection, "So, what did I miss?"

Or "What did you do today?"

"Ummm," I stammer, trying to muster a little enthusiasm. "Well, I just woke up a few minutes ago and now I'm drinking a cup of coffee."

I'd ask him how his day was and he'd tell me over the next hour about how they'd saved little girls from a brothel, or headed off human sacrifices by witch doctors, or put bad guys in prison. It's always good to hear his voice, but after we hung up, I'd need to convince myself all over again that the work I am doing matters, too. And you know what? It does.

On one trip to India, I knew from Bob's calls that a raid in a brothel area was going to take place that night. I was looking forward to hearing whether the team had success. The night before, almost a dozen little girls had been freed. It was late in India, which meant it was early in the morning when the phone rang.

"Hello, Maria?" I was expecting to hear Bob's voice but it was someone else's. After shaking the cobwebs off, I recognized it was Moses on the other end of the line. Instead of the cheerful guy I usually heard when he called, he sounded urgent.

"Moses, are you okay?" I asked, pressing the phone closer to my ear in hopes of hearing him better. Moses was speaking faster than normal and I couldn't catch more than every third word. I asked him to slow down so I could understand him better.

"Are you okay?" I repeated.

"Yes."

"Is Bob okay?"

Then came another rapid-fire set of words I couldn't understand.

"Moses! Slow down. Is Bob okay?" I asked, startled by the intense tone of my own voice.

"No," he replied.

I collapsed onto the stairs in our entryway. I felt helpless. "What happened?" I half shouted into the phone. A few understandable words trickled through about a raid, a mob, an attack, brothel owners stoning Bob and his friends, a hospital, and a jail in India. The call ended and that was all of the information I had.

I leaned up against the wall in the stairwell. I wasn't ready for this news, and I had no idea what I could do to help. I didn't have an emergency contact in India. Moses *was* my emergency contact. He was the one I could call if anything came up on my end. We didn't have a plan for what to do if anything happened on Bob's end. Clearly, Moses wasn't in the position to help either of us; he needed help, too. Sometimes being ready means traveling together and other times it means sending the people we love; but engagement involves risk, and risk requires sacrifice. Honestly, these are things I've spent most of my life trying to avoid. But I've also learned from Jesus that He doesn't want to shape me into a more fearful person; He wants to have us look more like Him.

Bob returned from the trip, as he always does and I was a little more ready for what God might have next for us. The beautiful thing is—we don't know what that will be. You don't either. Every day, we each get to decide if we will move toward the things that frighten us or move away from them. We decided as a family to continue to move toward those things that we can't control for one simple reason: We believe in the One who is in control of all of them.

When Bob sets out on one of his adventures, I get another opportunity to set out on one of my own—right where I am. Whether or not I go with him or stay at home, I'm a part of it, too. My faith gets stretched and challenged. The way I care for my husband on the opposite side of the world is much like the way I care for him when he's on the other side of the living room. I'm present, I'm supportive, and I'm confident that God's holding on to our family during difficult times, just as we're trying to reach out to others during theirs.

On that day and many others, all I could do was pray. We're all in that place at one time or another. Sometimes we have no idea what to pray for or how to pray. It gives me a great deal of comfort to know that our most desperate prayers don't need words.

As that day unfolded in what felt like slow motion, I received phone calls from Bob's close friends. Their encouragement during a time of tremendous ambiguity spoke volumes of the power of community in our lives. If you want to love someone well, love their family in a time of uncertainty. Their kind words helped shore me up during a time when I found myself questioning why Bob was doing these things overseas. One of them reminded me of this truth: "Not even the gates of hell can prevail against the will of God." I wrote it down on a Post-it and stuck it in my Bible that day.

If God is clear about one thing, it's this: What is good, true, right, and just will last. Everything else won't.

God points us in the direction of these things and whispers go, love, serve, help, clothe, and feed. Sure, go to India if that's where He leads, but if you're not sure, go across the street while you're waiting for more clarity. Don't get stuck getting ready. Go. Draw a one-hundred-foot circle around yourself and go love everybody inside it. Figure out what you're passionate about, what you're good at, and what will outlast you and then do a ton of that. Practice being ready to be used by God and the people around you.

Paul had some advice for his friends. He reminded them that Jesus would finish the good things they were doing. But we need to start it for Him to finish it. If we only run the races we know we'll win, it's no race at all.

What's your big dream? What's your beautiful ambition? Stop waiting. Put the lists away. Take it out of the spin cycle. Will it work? Who knows. We won't know how the race will turn out until we finish it, not before. God doesn't handicap us like horses at a race either. Don't look at who else is running the race; stay in your lane and keep your eyes on the finish line. Winning doesn't mean crossing the finish line in front of everyone else; it's being constantly ready to run in the direction of Jesus. If we're doing it correctly, this will always take us to the poor, the weak, and the helpless.

To "go" simply means to live. Are you ready? Are you finished spending all your time merely getting set?

Then go!

CHAPTER 15

Let Love Set the Table

There's a tradition around our house. It's been in place for a while now. We serve dinner on paper plates. Actually, we usually just do this when we don't want to do the dishes. When we do, someone will get the "star plate." That's the plate that has a small star drawn on the bottom of it. We shuffle the plates like a deck of cards so no one knows who's getting the star plate. Getting this plate is a big deal, because whoever ends up with it gets to pick what we have for dessert. It's really nothing other than getting to choose between a scoop of ice cream or a handful of grapes. But for the one who gets to choose, they're given the ultimate power and everyone knows it. It's all done in fun, but you should hear the paper plate trash talk before we discover who got the plate. What we like the most is that in the end, everyone wins.

Practicing hospitality right where we are with the people we love is always a good place to start giving away our love. Especially when we use what we have and do with it what we can. Whether we use paper plates or fancy china, no one really cares what the place settings look like if a person is sitting where they're loved. It's a reminder to me that we buy the plates, but love sets the table.

I have a friend whose favorite word is *with*. I bet that's one of God's favorite words, too. I can see why. God wanted to be *with* us, so He sent Jesus. He even named Him Immanuel, *God with us,* so that we would know He meant it. When Jesus left for heaven, He told His friends the Holy Spirit would be *with* them.

With. With. With.

The Bible is like a manual in that way, teaching us how to be with each other in the same way Jesus was with us: fully, completely, and sacrificially.

The concept of being *with* one another is both easy and difficult. At our core, I think we all want to be with the ones we love, in the same way Jesus was with His people. There are more than a few ways we do this, but hospitality is one that resonates best with me. The very nature of hospitality finds its footing in love.

Many of us put a lot of pressure on ourselves to be hospitable, but that pressure doesn't really belong—it's inconsistent with the goal. The world sets high standards, but in God's economy perfect hospitality is synonymous with tremendous love.

I have the same insecurities we all have. Maybe even more. Inviting people in isn't always easy for me. One time when my kids were young, we hosted the ambassador of a country in our home. When we heard he accepted our invitation, I was terrified. The ambassador and his family would be traveling to San Diego to see us, and they would be arriving in two weeks. I was honored they were coming, but our home was still a work in progress. My mind was spinning. I calculated whether there would be enough time to remodel the kitchen, lay down sod, grow a few new trees, paint the house, and repave the driveway. Perhaps. We didn't have much time. I imagined them pulling up in a black limousine adorned with little flags above the headlights.

I wondered if we would need to provide security.

Would they have guns? Would we need guns? I wasn't sure.

On top of thinking I needed to make the house perfect and their lives safe, I thought I'd better learn to cook something gourmet.

I wondered and worried about all of this for days. All the time, my insecurity level approached code red. Nothing in life had prepared me for this. I didn't have the proper training, prior experience, a butler, or a chef. All our family had was ourselves, a stack of paper plates, and a modest home. All we could really offer was our friendship and love. Deep down, I knew it would be enough.

Some time later, the ambassador and his family pulled into the driveway in a rented minivan. They looked like a family on vacation from Ohio. As it turns out, our guests weren't expecting us to be anything other than what we were when we first met. No one would have eaten any of the fancy food I thought I was supposed to prepare, and pizza was at the top of everyone's favorite food list. Who knew? When we're ourselves, it gives others the freedom to be who they are, too.

After dinner, our kids got out a bag of balloons, inflated them, and decorated the ambassador's seven-year-old son from head to toe. When they finished, they twisted even more balloons into the shape of a crown, a shield, and a sword. The look of delight on this young boy's face was priceless. I think the world needs more people covered in balloons. Love and laughter heals our souls and warms our hearts no matter who or where you are.

All of this was a good reminder to me that inviting people into our lives doesn't start with worry and stress. It starts with a desire for connection. Hospitality is always a matter of the heart; it's not the condition of our homes.

We always felt like it was important for our kids to have great table manners. In fact, for years we practiced them. We called it our "good manners night." The boys would pull out chairs for the girls and napkins were placed in laps. We got the silverware where it belonged and used the several forks in the correct order. The boys grumbled a little, but I knew they'd be glad someday when they went out on a date. Good manners night was always followed a few days later with "bad manners night." There would be no rules, no utensils, and lots of sloppy joe's and spaghetti eaten with bare hands just for fun. It's great to know all of the manners, but Jesus didn't ask His friends to just be polite with Him, He wanted them engaged. We wanted the same for our kids.

My favorite scene in the movie *Hook* is when Robin Williams sits down with the Lost Boys for dinner, but there isn't any food. They use their imaginations to fill their empty plates with mountains of turkey, mashed potatoes, and bread. The whole scene ends with a huge food fight. It's truly awesome to see everyone covered head to toe in a rainbow of colors. We can all lose our imaginations when it comes to serving dinner night after night. It's a lot more fun to mix it up. So for Thanksgiving one year, we did. We had a Lost Boys Thanksgiving Dinner.

We moved the dining room table out on the lawn, and everyone dressed in Lost Boy costumes. After eating a traditional Thanksgiving dinner, we had everyone close their eyes just like they did in the movie and told them to imagine mountains of colorful desserts. While their eyes were closed, we put huge big bowls of colorful Cool Whip on the table. We had them open their eyes and without any prompting from us, the best food fight this side of Plymouth Rock broke out.

For years, I was stuck in the trap that our family occasions required me to toil for days in the kitchen. The idea had cut such a deep groove in my brain that it separated me from most of the family fun. I knew I'd gone around the bend when I was more concerned about whether the potatoes were baking than if our hearts were growing. For years, on Christmas Eve, I bought into the lie that I needed to fill our house with the aroma of Christmas goose, seafood cioppino, and plum pudding. It was as if I expected Julia Child or Ina Garten to join us for dinner—holding a scorecard. I had forgotten that Jesus isn't hoping for us to be celebrity chefs; He just wants us to be available.

I knew something had to change, so we asked our kids what they thought would make Christmas Eve even more special for them. Their answer wasn't that they wanted fancy food. They wanted In-N-Out burgers. If you haven't had one of these burgers before, fix that soon. The kids' honesty was freeing. I no longer felt the pressure to be something I'm not, or do things that took me away from my family. Besides, it didn't actually matter that much to them anyway. Now, on Christmas Eve, our house is filled with the aroma of double-double cheeseburgers, French fries, and milk shakes.

I love pomp and circumstance more than food, so we still set the table in a magnificent display of Christmas china, Waterford crystal glasses, glowing candles, cut greens, and white linen napkins. Bob learned how to fold napkins into fancy shapes during college when he was a waiter for one brief night. He says the napkin looks like a partridge in a pear tree. It doesn't of course, but we love him, so we say it does.

Everyone is given an English party popper. The kind that comes with a tissue paper crown, a tiny toy, and a clever joke. They sound like small firecrackers when they're pulled apart, which the boys like a lot. Paper flies everywhere and each year we try not to light the tablecloth on fire.

Because we like being together around the table on Christmas Eve, grabbing takeout like we're at the beach and setting the table like it's a banquet fit for the King gives us more time to be with each other and to celebrate together.

For as long as our kids lived at home, most nights we made it a point to have dinner together. When Bob travels, he makes it a priority to be home for dinner whenever he can. The first thing he does when someone asks him to come speak to them isn't to find out how to get there, it's to figure out how to get home for supper. If someone asks these days, "Where's Bob?" the answer I'm usually able to give is, "He's on his way home."

We're made from the factory to run home to each other.

One time when I was away, Bob took the kids to the grocery store and told them whatever they picked out is what they'd have for dinner. To this day, they gleefully recount the menu of Surge soda, marshmallow PEEPS, and canned SPAM for the main course. They saved the *really* unhealthy stuff for dessert. They even set the table and invited our neighbor Laurie to join them. Bob knew one nutritionally devastating meal wouldn't kill the kids. In fact, the memory did more to nurture a family value of fun, adventure, and unlikely conversations around the table than a mountain of broccoli.

I've never stopped to count how many meals we've served around our table. I bet it's a lot. I couldn't tell you every detail about every conversation or the food served. But I know with certainty, the time together around the table has shaped us. It's where we share our hearts and our dreams, not just our food.

The table is also a place to be together during more serious times. It's not a place of discipline. It's hard to swallow food when you feel like you're in trouble, so those conversations are taken somewhere else. I've heard how good questions make good conversations, and good listening makes everyone feel heard. Sharing real and vulnerable stuff brings people closer together. The table is a safe place where more than food is passed around.

Our daughter's hardest day in junior high was when she learned that a friend had taken her own life. It was hard for any of us to wrap our heads around what had happened, and, understandably, Lindsey was very sad. That night around the dinner table, we took time to share our thoughts and feelings. Bob talked to the boys about how they could care for their sister while she was sad. He said it was a good idea to be incredibly kind and empathic when someone is sad. He suggested if they saw her crying and didn't know what to do, they could always get her a tissue, give her a hug, or both. What we say around the table gives us context for what happens out in the world.

Jesus set a great example of hospitality and intentionality during the Last Supper. He served a simple meal of bread, wine, and heartfelt conversations. All of which took place around a table where everyone was invited. We don't know who set it, but we know everyone was welcome. Even a friend who would soon let Him down. Simple is good. Safe is good. It's what Jesus did and it's what we should do.

The formula I use includes my favorite recipes and all-white dinner dishes. The table is usually set with bottles of pomegranate juice from Trader Joe's and San Pellegrino water with slices of lemons and limes. There are always candles and fresh-cut greens from the yard. These simple details are the foundations that set the scene and anchor the memories we make together.

The table is not only a place to eat, it's a place to learn about life and each other. It's also a place to invite people to leave their mark. There is a longstanding tradition at our home. After dinner we invite everyone who has broken bread at our table to climb underneath and sign it. Long after the guests have gone home, a piece of them stays with us. Much like the early Acts church, who broke bread together and had things in common, we make our table one of those things we have in common. Don't overcomplicate it. When gathering together is rooted in love, free of unnecessary stress or self-serving motivations, bonds are formed, hearts are mended, and lives are changed forever.

We put a priority on togetherness. It's a fundamental value for our family. Dinnertime is a good time for us to meet that need. It doesn't always look like a scene from a Norman Rockwell painting; it's way better—it looks like us. Some nights can feel like herding cats around a food trough. Those were the nights we needed to remind ourselves why we decided it was a good idea in the first place. For us, dinner will always be more than the food. Dinner could burn in the pan, but our connection with each other still fills us. It's about being consistent in taking the time to stop, reflect, unwind, and be thankful for the time together.

We don't always get it right around our table and you won't always get it right around yours. But we still meet there. Keep meeting around yours, too. Be *with* each other. Do it often. Do it intentionally. Be there together fully, completely, sacrificially, and don't forget to bring a few balloons. You may not end up with a star under your plate, but you'll have the aroma of love around your table.

CHAPTER 16

Tossing Rocks

We grow our food in Canada.

I learned early on what it takes to make a garden grow. I thought it was just dirt, water, and a little sun. If all you want are a few carrots, that will actually work. But if you really want to produce something you can live off of, there's a little more to it. A couple of the lessons I've learned have provided beautiful metaphors to help me understand my faith a little better.

Here's what I mean.

When I first started gardening, I thought my biggest obstacle would be the rocks I found in the soil. I thought they were the things getting in the way of my efforts to dig the right holes for my plants. Yet, looking up at the granite cliffs around me, I saw giant cedar trees growing out of sheer granite walls. I saw how a small volunteer strawberry plant thrives in the gravel and how a full-grown maple tree proudly displays its leaves faithfully even in the harshest of conditions. I had heard an old gardening tip that suggests the way to get the best results is to dig a ten-dollar hole for a two-dollar plant. I don't know if that's true or not. What I do know is that the soil we prepare for the ones we love will cost us the most. Preparing soil that someone can grow in is hard work, but it's not all the work. Preparing your own soil is where the most important tilling is done.

Our job isn't to dig other people's holes; it's to dig our own. Certainly, help them if they invite you to, but don't trespass. When we tend to our own soil, the roots of everyone planted near us will find their depth. Dig deep where you've been planted. Find the good soil and dig there. Will you hit a couple rocks as you do? Probably. Don't worry about it. Keep digging. Where we dig the deepest is where love will grow the best.

I love the look, the smell, and everything about freshly tilled dirt. I would rather have a garden of only good clean dirt than one filled with overgrown, unwanted, or unhealthy plants. Turning over the soil helps me get to what I want, but it's not enough. When farmers only cultivate the top couple feet and a half over and over again, what forms is a rock-hard layer of dirt called a "plough pan." It's the dirt that doesn't get touched. It looks like dirt and from the top the field looks well tended to, but a couple feet down from the surface it becomes as hard as concrete.

What happens in huge Midwest fields will happen in our lives too if we only till what's on the surface. Our roots won't go deep and we'll stop growing if we let a plough pan develop.

To get through this hard layer, every once in a while a tractor drags huge teeth through the field called a chisel plough. It has two purposes. First, to get deep and second, to break up the soil that has become hard. We can't break up the hard stuff if we won't go deep, and we can't go deep without getting out the chisel plough every now and again. If you've just been tilling the top couple feet in your life, find a deeper plough.

It wasn't until I had the responsibility of raising kids that I paid much attention to the soil they were planted in and the need to prune, toss, and let things go. I wasn't concerned about the effects of what was getting stuck in the dark corners of my life. If it wasn't bothering anyone else, I'd let it be. When the responsibility of raising human beings became my life's work, I started to care more than I ever thought was possible about the soil surrounding the kids. Unhealthy relationships, bad habits, and negative self-talk weren't doing me any favors or helping the people around me. Having kids made digging up my own soil a priority. I realized I needed to get rid of some rocks of my own and dig a little deeper.

When the kids were young, Bob and I tossed the busyness of outside distractions in order to protect our home life. We took time off from volunteering in youth ministry, cut down on evening events for a period of time to give consistency to our schedule, and we eliminated a couple good things to make room for three great things: Lindsey, Richard, and Adam. Family memories mean more to me than personal accomplishments. Both are good, but on a priority scale, there are seasons when spending time with the family will always mean more to me. It's an investment worth making.

Over time if we ignore unresolved issues, like weeds in the garden, it won't take long before it will become wildly overgrown. Just like the climbing vines on garden walls, unattended issues in our families can take over the whole house if we don't tend to them regularly.

When I started raising kids, I had no idea what kind of wife and mother I would be. No one really does, I suppose. Deep down I hoped I would become the person I had dreamed of, but the truth is, I didn't know who that was. Most of us don't have a lot of role models. I watched the wives and mothers around me. I paid close attention to how other women led their lives. I saw how they spoke to the ones they loved and pursued the dreams they had. I wasn't critical of what I saw, yet something in my heart kept whispering that it could be done differently. I believe we get two childhoods, the one we grow up with, and the one we give to our kids. I was determined to do whatever it took to cultivate good family soil, dig some deep holes, toss the rocks, and let love grow.

I've heard stories of mothers lifting cars off of their children to save a child's life. I was sure I wanted that kind of love for my own kids. I didn't think it would take supernatural powers to do this, but extraordinary love. I wondered if I were capable of that kind of love. I think we all do. It turns out I've never had to lift any cars over my head, but on more than a few occasions I have felt the overwhelming need to protect or advocate for my family. In those times, it surprised me to see how quick my instincts could be. I'm convinced there's no swifter reflex known to mankind than the love of a mother or father protecting their young. It's exactly how God feels about us when we're in danger.

Several summers ago when our family was in Canada, a huge bear was in our garden eating its way through our blackberry bushes. It came onto the deck looking for food just outside the kitchen window. I chased it off with a paintball gun loaded with neon pink paintballs. I shot twice and missed twice. As the bear ran away, I squeezed off one last shot and I hit it on the butt. There was pink paint everywhere. It was like furry art in motion as the bear ran away down the path.

I love animals and respect that we're in their forest, not the reverse. I knew the black bear had been hanging around the Lodge looking for food for a few weeks and I hadn't done anything. On that day he became a danger to my family; he crossed the line. It surprised me how fiercely protective I could be when the kids safety was threatened. Ten minutes later a call came over the radio from the Young Life camp next door.

"There's a bear in camp!"

"What color is its butt?" I asked with a laugh, suspecting it was the same bear.

Figure out what is endangering your family and mark it. Know what it is when it climbs up on your deck and do what you need to in order to keep your family safe.

———————

When one of our kids was heartbroken at the end of a relationship, I knew we needed to figure out how to offer love, support, and respect. It was a significant time in our lives. Even so, we had a ton to celebrate as a family. Bob had finished writing a book, the boys were doing well in college, and Lindsey was just out of graduate school and had her first teaching job.

There was an old duffel bag of things that was a reminder of the hurt one of my children felt. I love what a friend of ours, Henry Cloud, says, "Time does *not* heal all things, just ask an infected tooth. Time *plus* doing the right thing heals what hurts." Everyone involved was moving on down their own paths, but to me the bag of stuff symbolized the past and I realized it was keeping me stuck. I was ready to accept the reality that some people can be in our hearts but not in our lives. This old bag was like a rock that needed to be dug out of my soil.

It was a rainy day in Canada and I had the afternoon alone. I put on my raincoat, tugged the heavy old duffel bag off of the closet shelf, hauled it out the front door, down the stairs, and across the boat ramp. I rolled the bag off the dock and into the metal hull of a boat my family affectionately named the *Sweet Maria*. Pausing to acknowledge the irony in the moment, I thought, *Sweet Maria? Not today.*

I headed for the deepest possible spot in the inlet, put the engine in neutral, and threw the bag overboard. It landed with a splash.

I had done it. I had figured out what had kept me stuck and got rid of it. It's one of the steps we each need to make in order to move forward.

I welled up with pride, but it was only short lived. A boat length away, the bag resurfaced. I let out a groan. "You have got to be kidding me" I remember saying out loud to the empty inlet. The bag was actually floating, not sinking. That's not at all what I was expecting. Yet this is what we all experience when we're on the path to a breakthrough.

We get rid of what we thought was hanging us up and it resurfaces a short distance away. It was as if it were tied to me; and in fact, metaphorically, it was.

How could something so heavy, something that took so much effort to get rid of actually come back to the surface? I quickly lunged over the edge of the boat and pulled the bag back toward me. With my heart pounding, fingers freezing, I fumbled for the zipper and opened the bag just enough to release any trapped air. It still wouldn't sink. I gave the zipper another tug—this time hoping to let in a little water—when, suddenly, ice-cold water rushed into the bag, and an old tennis shoe flew out with such force it made me jump. This has happened to all of us. We try to discard what's holding us back, but sometimes it takes a couple tries.

My attempt to sink the bag wasn't working, so I hauled the soggy mess back into the boat and made my way to shore to come up with another plan. I realized that the only way to sink the bag was to add a few rocks of my own. We can't really put things behind us by getting rid of someone else's stuff. We need to get rid of a couple rocks of our own. It might be our pride or our dominance or our desire for control. Sometimes when I think something is holding me back, I figure out it's me.

Heading back out to sea, I noticed a pod of seals had gathered in the exact spot of my first attempt at a burial at sea. "Oh thank goodness," I mumbled to myself, glad that I wasn't alone. I wondered how I could enlist them in the effort, but bailed on the idea when I realized I had no fish food to sweeten the deal. The seals held their shiny heads above water and kept a close watch as I dumped the bag overboard one last time. I had silent witnesses this time of my willingness to add my own rocks I'd been carrying around.

This time, with the added weight of what I needed to let go of in my life, the bag sank beneath the water's surface and slowly descended to its watery grave. The seals disappeared with it, and I imagined them following the strange black mass to the bottom of the sea. My job was finished. I stood up in the boat and dried my wet hands on my jeans.

The inlet had never seemed more peaceful. That's the way it is when we make small breakthroughs. The gray sky and low wispy clouds looked like cotton candy snagged on the tips of the huge cedar pines that grew out of the rocky edge of Patrick's Point in the distance. I took a photo of the inlet. It's a reminder that sometimes we find strength by letting go, but we don't let go of much until we add the ballast we're holding on to.

We can't always save the day for the ones we love. Despite our best efforts, glasses of milk spill, fingers will get caught in doors, strings on balloons will come undone, college midterms are failed, and relationships will stumble.

to protect the ones we love from heartbreak, ointments, and adversity, but in this life it is unavoidable. I think God made it this way for a reason. He uses these times to realize our absolute need for Him and to till our own soil a little more.

Tossing rocks into the water has always been a tradition for our friends at the Lodge. It's a way of symbolizing something they've been carrying around for years, and no longer has a place in their life. It's a tangible sign of letting go. I've thrown my share of rocks. Probably a couple wheelbarrows full. There's something incredibly freeing about naming the things that are hanging us up, claiming the promises of God over them, and then letting them go. I laugh to myself when the news talks about rising ocean levels. I've always suspected it's not global warming, but all of my rocks that are to blame. There's still plenty of things I need to let go of. We all do. Just when I've let go of one or two, three or four new ones show up. I used to be surprised when this happened, but I'm not anymore. Like Forrest Gump famously said in the movie, "Sometimes, I guess there just aren't enough rocks."

Jesus left His hometown. Mary left her reputation. Moses and his people left Egypt. Noah left everything. All of these heroes in the Bible let go of something in order to grab hold of something else. They got rid of what was convenient to make room for what was necessary. People who live with purpose, obedience, resolve, and meaning are constantly renewing themselves by leaving things behind.

Tossing rocks can represent an ending, but it can also represent a new beginning, too. It can represent a renewed resolve to embrace the hope of new possibilities for our lives, or making a commitment to move toward a better version of ourselves. Anyone can throw rocks at people. It just takes an arm and an attitude. Getting rid of the things that are separating us from God or from people takes humility and courage. Letting go of the things that no longer serve us makes room for new things that will. It makes both the soil and our holes better to plant in. When we have the guts to do this, more will grow in our lives and the lives of the people we love.

Go find a pond. It's time to get rid of a couple things you've been carrying around. You know what it is. Throwing it into the water may be enough, but if it won't sink, add a couple rocks of your own.

CHAPTER 17

Finding Rest

We all have one thing in common: *We need rest.*

Sometimes it's deep rest and sometimes it's brief. We all get what we can, where we can, and when we can. But here's the thing: We're settling for getting the rest we're able to get, but not the rest we actually need.

Teenagers stay up all night and then sleep all day on sofas, under desks, and in hammocks stretched between trees. People with start-up companies and school finals do the same. We're not the only ones with weird resting habits. I've read that giraffes only sleep twenty minutes a day. It's the same for a couple new moms I know. Albatross sleep while they fly.

I'm not kidding.

I'm not really sure why we try to get rest in the peculiar ways we do. I suppose we're all just trying to cope with the competing claims on our time. Birds have to fly and giraffes need to stay awake. We're all just trying to do the best we can to manage the circumstances we are dealt. So we cope with the hailstorm of activities and responsibilities we've agreed to, while forfeiting the rest we need.

The world tells us to get some sleep, take a break, or go on a vacation; but we know it doesn't really mean it because at the same time it sells us more than nine million bottles of energy shots per week. We put a premium on over-amped, over-caffeinated, high-achieving lives and miss what we were designed by God to need the most, which is solid rest. We all have seasons in life when that isn't possible; but like *The Lion, the Witch and the Wardrobe,* when it's always winter but never Christmas, the seasons of calm are constantly deferred by us. Jesus' message to His friends was simple. He told them to let Christmas come a little earlier in their lives, to come away with Him and find rest.

When our son Richard was little, he could fall asleep anywhere: on a boat, in a plane, and even under the table after a holiday dinner. It was hard to tell sometimes if he was awake or asleep. He could be standing up, looking forward, but he would actually be out cold. Only his glazed-over eyes would tell the truth. I'd look at his face, nudge his shoulder, and say, "Hey buddy, are you okay?" while holding his wrist to check for a pulse. One night, Bob even found him sleepwalking in our neighbor's yard wearing nothing but his boxers. It was more than a little weird.

Yet, it's not unlike how a lot of us go through life. We might have more than boxers on, but much of the time when our eyes are open, we're actually asleep to what's going on around us. The opposite is true as well. When we do find our way to bed at night, our eyes might be closed, but we're not actually resting at all. The activities, uncertainties, and complex relationships we're trying to figure out and balance are as loud as a bunch of roosters crowing, constantly bidding us to abandon rest. We will never find our purpose in exhaustion.

The truth is, it's hard to get what we really need, so we settle for what we can easily get. When our kids were growing up, I found small islands of solace while sitting quietly in my car waiting for the school bell to ring. It wasn't enough, but it was the few coveted minutes I needed to make the transition from rushing around getting things done to reconnecting with the kids again. I thought all of this might change as the kids grew up, but the older we all got, the busier we got. Eventually, we learned to substitute activity and productivity for what we needed much more—rest.

I learned something when we were remodeling our home. A piece of plywood is actually stronger than a solid piece of wood. Here's the reason: Plywood is made of lots of thin layers of wood with glue holding them all together. The direction of the grain in the plywood is rotated ninety degrees with each layer added. The glue triples the strength of the wood. We're all like plywood in many ways. The thin pieces of wood in our lives are the things we value the most and what we're good at. Rest is the glue that keeps all of these things we value together. Forget the glue in our lives and all we have to work with is a bunch of thin scraps of wood.

It isn't just something we do when we're asleep either. It's a place we can go when we're awake. We all have places of rest. Some of these places we find and some we make. Find your place. It can be beside a small stream, at a park, under a bridge, or at the end of an old oak tree limb. Find that place and go there often. Make it yours. Claim it. Tell it you'll be right back when you leave.

In addition to finding places of quiet disconnection, we can also make them. I've worked hard to make our home a place of rest not only for me, but also for the people I love. I knew it was working when I saw it written on my kids' expressions when they were young and living at home. I still see it as they've grown and come back home just to hang out. Resting places are safe places. When the people I love walk through the door, I don't hit them with a list of problems or issues or suggestions or complaints. I welcome them with the ambiance of a warm home embroidered with peace. Do the same and you'll find it, too. Let it spread like a cold in your family. Be picky about the words you say and the advice you give, and your family will find the rest they need.

I place a high value on making beautiful spaces where our family lives. My goal is to create an atmosphere where everyone can thrive. I do this by doing the best I can with what I have. It never mattered to me if my home was a tent, a doublewide trailer, or a tiny apartment. If it were one of these, I'm sure it would be a great looking one with the best one-dollar posters and two-dollar pillows I could find. More important than all of the decorations we add is the safety of the place we make. Each of us finds our deepest rest in places that feel secure. Making our home safe didn't mean boarding up the trap door I'm delighted to tell you we have in our closet. It means not having relational trap doors in our living spaces. Our family can say what they need to say without wondering if the floor is going to drop out from under them. Say fewer obvious things and more encouraging ones.

When Bob walks through the front door after a fierce conflict he's managed as a trial lawyer, or after a long stretch of travel days, I don't offer him advice on the cases he's handling and he doesn't offer me advice on what I should be doing. I wouldn't know what to say to him and he wouldn't know what to say to me. I also don't greet him with a wrench and tell him the faucet is leaking. Instead, I give him something I know he needs—a breather. We'll get to the drip after he gets to his rest.

Rest lets us focus. We can wish for fewer distractions, but the cruel reality is, the longer we live, the more we'll have. We can ask God to bring fewer problems our way, too. Go ahead, try it. I've been asking for that for years, but it hasn't worked. Rest doesn't just give us the ability to cope with the challenges we face but, more importantly, to understand them.

Rest isn't our keeper; it's our teacher. It prepares us to deal with the most painful and difficult challenges we'll ever face. It isn't found just in the things we do or don't do. Often, it's best experienced in the familiar rhythms of our lives. The sights, smells, and sounds in our places of calm have a way of nurturing our spirits.

I buy the same candle from our favorite hotel every time we're within driving distance of it. The reason is simple. It reminds us to rest so I light it in our home in the evenings. Finding the sights and smells of rest heals our souls and fills our hearts. Again, this is because it isn't just something we find; it's a place we create. We relax where we feel safe. Find those places in your life and make it your rhythm to go there often.

This idea of creating a place of rest wasn't our idea, of course. It was Jesus who told His friends they needed rest. The Bible says His friends were running around so much they didn't even have time to eat or sleep. Most of us can relate. They had traveled the countryside teaching, healing, and doing miracles. The work Jesus' friends were doing was good, important, and life-changing stuff, to be sure. They restored sight to the blind, helped the crippled walk, and brought life where it had slipped away. Your work is important, too. If you want to keep doing it well, get some rest. Jesus invited these friends to "Come aside to a quiet secluded place and rest." He knew what the disciples needed to follow Him more closely. It wasn't more information, it wasn't more time together, and it wasn't another Bible study; it was more rest. The same is true for us.

People who accomplish much, rest well. The Bible actually says a great deal about a theology of rest. We rise, we do, we rest, we repeat. Hard work and good rest aren't mutually exclusive. They complement one another. We need to help these two seemingly opposing ideas learn to play well in the sandbox together in our lives. People who learn to play hard and rest well see more waterfalls, sunsets, and rainbows. Go find yours.

Over the years, we've expanded our invitation to come and rest, beyond just our family, to people who are shaping culture in our world. Some of these people lead organizations, others write books, and make movies. Some sing opera, others can shred electric guitars, and a few write the worship songs we all sing at church. Still others are leaders of countries. They may lead through democratically held elections or through rebel uprisings, but they influence millions. All of these people who come have one thing in common. They're all just as beat as the high school kid volunteering at the camp washing dishes. While their weeks look different from the outside, they need the same things on the inside. Rest.

Whether it is short or long, we all need the kind of respite where our responsibilities are lifted and the pressures of what we *do* are replaced with remembering who we *are*. Make that place in your life or find one that someone else has made, but get there often. Places of rest are holy, they're sacred, and they're rare. Stop writing bad checks with your life you can't cover without some rest. Find your place and go there—often.

CHAPTER 18

The Fire

Before the Lodge existed, our favorite family vacation was to go boating in the Pacific Northwest. The kids were just learning how to swim, so all of our family pictures have the kids buckled into huge red life jackets. Our kids looked like they were in the Coast Guard. We learned a lot about boating on those trips, but we also learned a lot about living in close quarters as a family. We all adapt to the environments we spend the most time in. There is good and bad in this, I suppose. We're all reflections or reactions. We end up reflecting those things that appeal to us the most and reacting to the things that don't.

Let me give you a couple examples. If you grew up in a family where there were a lot of raised voices, you'll probably react by avoiding people who raise their voices. If there was a lot of chaos in your life when you were young, you might be living a very ordered life now. You're a reaction to those inputs. We're also reflections. If you are around kind, generous people, you'll probably be kind and generous. If you have experienced the power of love and forgiveness in your life, you'll probably give away a lot of both. Here's the thing: We get to decide what kind of reflection or reaction we will be. We can react by lashing out, or we can be beautiful reflections. We can reflect the angst we felt or the grace we've received.

Being in close proximity to one another feels very normal to each of us in our family. Our home isn't big. Most of the time, you'll find us all huddled in the same small room. It's not even a conscious decision. We just kind of end up there. I think I know why. We're reflections. We travel together. We do projects around the house together. We wash cars together. We walk through the grocery store in a pack. It's not even conscious. It really got weird on a trip through London when someone needed to make a phone call, and we all tried to climb into one of the red phone booths together. One of the reasons we're close as a family is because we want to be close to each other.

───────

When the kids were young, we spent our summers helping out together at a camp. We made videos to give to the campers at the end of the week so they could remember and share the highlights from the best week of their lives.

We lived on our small boat together, took videos together during the day, and edited them together each night. It was more than just doing things together that brought us close; it was doing things for other people that made it purposeful.

One summer, while we were at the camp, we heard the roar of helicopters overhead. We learned they were coming for the trees. Each first growth cedar tree has as much as tens of thousands of dollars of lumber in it. The logging company who owned the land in this pristine inlet had begun logging it. It was like all the worst parts of the movie *Avatar*. We felt compelled to protect camp and the beauty of the inlet, so over the next many years we bought most of the forest around the camp. The original plan didn't include building anything on the property we had protected, but one afternoon Bob and I were walking around in the forest and started wondering out loud if we could make a place for the volunteers from camp to come and find the rest they needed. Bob said that with enough dynamite, we could make a really big flat spot in the almost vertical terrain—so we did.

For the next twenty years, we built the Lodge on that property.

Our most enduring memories of time together were made there. The kids learned to serve the guests, grow a garden, drive landing crafts, run excavators, fly a seaplane, and move the rocks. They helped build a hydroelectric plant and roads and buildings when they weren't wakeboarding or exploring. The Lodge became one of the places our family grew. Figuratively and literally. This was where Richard and Ashley spent many summers together before they were married, and the Lodge was where Lindsey and Jon celebrated their wedding.

Leaders from various countries have come to the Lodge and resolved some of their differences. We had some good guys, some bad guys, and a few who were undecided come up. Before everyone left, they would sign peace agreements between themselves on the flags of their respective countries. For the next decade and a half, dozens of countries were represented. The flags were stacked high inside the Lodge when not hanging proudly from the top of one of the many flag poles in anticipation of another visit from a countryman.

We brought up many of the people who have shaped our culture, too. Some of these people played rock-and-roll and others violins. Some wrote books or poems or made movies. Quite a few led large organizations and a couple won Olympic gold. Some succeeded at great things but failed at the most basic things in life.

No matter who came, all they had received from us was an invitation, nothing more. A few of the people who were invited wanted more details. We understood, of course, and it was a reasonable thing to ask for. We didn't make them feel bad when they asked, we just knew they probably wouldn't be coming. We liked the way Jesus did it. He didn't give a lot of details when He invited people to come with Him. They either came or they didn't. He didn't talk about where they were staying, what they were eating, or who else was coming either. The reason was simple. It wasn't a business trip Jesus was inviting them on; it was an adventure.

Every couple years, we put a coat of stain on the logs at the Lodge. It's a big job and takes two guys several months to complete. Bob and the boys have done it a couple times. This year, we hired a large painting contractor to go up and put one last coat of stain on the Lodge. We got a call that they had arrived late in the day and had worked for two hours before cleaning up for the day.

At midnight, Bob woke up to see Adam standing by our bed in San Diego. He had come to let us know that he got a message that the Lodge was on fire. We don't know what happened. We'll leave that to the experts. Did the painters throw some oily rags together in the bag at the back door at the end of the day? Did those rags spontaneously combust a few hours later? It appears so. Either way, twenty years of our life's work was erased in less than two hours.

––––––––

The fire at the Lodge was biblical. There were hardly even ashes left by the time it was over. It was like Sodom and Gomorrah, but nobody living there had done anything wrong. Everything I treasured the most had been incinerated. For all of the terrible losses, the worst one was that the one place in the world where I felt truly safe had been taken away from me.

After the fire, nothing in life made sense to me. The only thing that felt real was being with Bob, the kids, my faith in God, and the hope that someday this unthinkable reality would become something beautiful. The pain has ebbed somewhat, but honestly, I'm still not there yet. Some days are good and other days I bounce between hurt and disbelief. In other words, I'm in the middle, somewhere between the pain and the hope. It's the place where most of us live out our lives. It's not a comfortable place, but it's a familiar one.

I've never put a headlamp on and explored deep inside caves. I might be afraid of what I would find down there. But actually, it's the fear of even getting there that's even harder for me. The fact is, most of us don't have circumstances come up in our lives that cause us to enter our own caves. Sometimes it takes something massive to throw us down the hole. As much as I would have preferred not to go, it was the fire that got me to the bottom of my cave. It was dark and scary and I wasn't happy to be there. That said, because I seemed to have little choice in it, I thought I'd look around and see what I would find.

Within weeks of the fire, I realized something had shifted deep inside of me. The trauma from the fire, the loss, the feeling of not knowing how to make sense of it, all this caused emotions to bubble up to the surface. This unwanted cocktail of memories made my grief even more complicated; I really couldn't tell what was going on or where those feelings were coming from. As a child, I had learned to bury feelings I didn't understand. But now, a whole life full of feelings had arrived in the cave exposed by the fire, and I knew I couldn't ignore them anymore.

I had nightmares about flames and fire. Where I would normally light a candle or the fireplace at night, I couldn't even look at an open flame. I would wake in a panic, my heart racing most nights. I'd get up to shake the image away, but it didn't work. Was I going crazy? I told myself I was okay, but the fact was, I wasn't. This was more grief than I could handle, and I knew I needed to get help.

I've learned over the years that it's worth doing the hard work to get to a healthy place.

To get the help I needed, I went to place called Onsite. It's located just outside of Nashville, Tennessee. It's a beautiful therapeutic retreat center owned and run by people we know and love. It offers programs and workshops led by some of the world's greatest therapists who help people get unstuck. They have experienced counselors who help people navigate the twisty roads trauma leads us down

from time to time. Bob went with me, and we met with
Bill and Laurie, an amazing couple whom we have loved
for years. Both of them had spent time at the Lodge. I spent
most of my time with Laurie who hasn't just been a good
friend over the years, but a wise one. The two of us sat on
the thick carpet floor in our own private room.

I thought I was there to talk about the Lodge fire, but
it turns out I couldn't have been more wrong. When Laurie
asked me why the Lodge was important to me, I told her it
was the only place where I felt truly safe in the world.

"Hmm, has there been a time in your life you haven't
felt safe?" She asked.

I paused, took a giant gulp of air like a carp who had
just been scooped out of the lake, and huge messy tears just
started flowing. I wasn't really sure why at first. That's the
way our emotions are. Sometimes the reasons don't find
connection with the emotions until someone helps us connect the dots. We spent the next few days unpacking things
from decades ago, not just weeks ago. Laurie was a safe and
trusted guide in the cave I was at the bottom of. She gave
me the courage I've never had to light a torch and explore
why I hadn't ever really felt safe. I think we figured it out.

———

One of my earliest childhood memories was being
dropped off to spend the night with one of my relatives.

I don't remember ever before spending the night there or ever again afterward. My parents must have had something they needed to do because I was told I just needed to stay there that night. The house was quiet and sterile with nothing in it for a child to play with. After I had crawled into a strange bed and the lights were out, my relative came in to tell me my mom had called and said to be sure that I hadn't gone to bed in my underwear. I don't remember what happened next, but I am sure I was molested. Nothing about my life seemed the same again. The next day, it seemed as if all the colors in the world had changed after that night.

When I finished recalling my memory, Laurie finished my last sentence with a knowing hug and said, ". . . and so the Lodge became your safe place."

Keeping secrets takes it toll. I was relieved and exhausted to finally share mine. We called in Bob and Bill and I told them my story. As Bob sat listening, he held my hand tightly, nodded compassionately, and with an abundance of empathy let me know he was with me.

When I was done, there was a long silence. Then Bob told me how sad and sorry he was that this had happened; but if it took the fire to unearth the pain of my past, he would let the Lodge burn down all over again. His sentiment made me cry even more. Bob then said something that brought the first tension-breaking laugh. He said he wished he knew where this relative, who had long ago died, was buried so he could dig him up and kill him again.

I had my Bible with me and a few old family photos were tucked in its pages. One included a rare photo with this man standing in the background. I asked if we could use the fire pit at Onsite to burn the photo. It seemed both fitting and symbolic.

As the flames curled the photo into a wispy ball of ash, I knew I no longer needed to fear the fire that took the Lodge or my past the fire had exposed. Grieving the loss of the Lodge hasn't completely gone away. I'll probably be sad about it my whole life to some degree. But I know I am not stuck. I am learning to use the fire to bring light to the cave.

CHAPTER 19

The Chalkboard

For the first few years of our life together, Bob and I were collecting all the parts that would make up our family. The formula looked simpler than it was. Get married, find a place to live, have a job, and add babies. We hadn't really stopped to think about things like how to actually parent, like instilling values, and building character. We knew of course, these were at the core of what we needed to do. We felt like we were starting from scratch, living a general plan to the best of our abilities. We knew we loved each other, our kids, and God. We sort of knew what part of the country we wanted to live in, and we thought we knew what it would take to feed us all.

Those first few years were really hectic even while they were a lot of fun. It seemed that every couple of years we moved, fixed up the next house, and sold it. It was really hard yet rewarding work. With babies and busy lives, I started to feel like life was happening to us rather than the reverse. Unfortunately, more often than not, we found ourselves reacting to the next big event instead of living life with intention, reason, and purpose.

A stable and abundant home life is what I wanted deep down. A home full of people who practiced love, joy, peace, patience, and understanding, until we got it right, even if it took a lifetime to figure out how. I wanted a place where people felt nurtured, where exploring, adventuring, trying, and failing were supported. I envisioned a home where gathering for meals not only filled our stomachs but also nurtured our souls, and where we'd rally when one of us got sick or suffered or struggled. What I desired most was an environment where laughter and music hung in the air, where the flames of creativity were fanned and the fires lit by fear, judgment, and condemnation were snuffed out swiftly, and where everyone was safe from emotional trip wires and landmines. In short, I wanted my family to live where we could serve God, each other, and be able to say wholeheartedly to everyone entering it, *Welcome Home*.

We've come a long way since then. After Bob and I returned from an event recently, I walked into our kitchen and put down my overnight bag. I looked up at a chalkboard that had been hanging in our kitchen for twenty years. The big bold letters simply read: *Welcome Home*. To us, this is more than just an empty phrase or platitude from a Home Goods store; it was a declaration built on hundreds of choices and dreams. That night, its sentiment touched me deeply, as it has so many times before. I let out a deep sigh of relief as I relaxed into the reality of being home. Words of sincere welcome always have this kind of effect on a soul in need of rest.

The words *Welcome Home* still hang over our family like a perpetual banner. With three adult children and a husband who travels to encourage people all over the world, it reminds me that our home is both a launching pad and a landing place. It's a place to receive and release love, where our lives, with all the successes and failures, are welcomed. The words are more than a phrase; it's our anthem. As a family, we got to this place the old-fashioned way; we worked hard to make room for love, patience, and kindness. There's been a ton of laughter and more than a few mistakes and sadness, too.

Under the same roof of protection, I've started to notice there's a new season of life taking form. In the olden days when our kids were young, being at home was the norm while being away was rare. Back then, homework papers, school bags, and dirty tennis shoes were left just inside the back door. The house was abuzz with activity. We had a landline for a house phone that always rang, music playing in the background, and the doorbell chiming. These were the soundtracks for five different people (and a dog). The chalkboard in the kitchen mostly highlighted celebrations, funny quotes, drawings, or words of encouragement back then. My favorite, especially during the kids' finals week, was a quote from their school librarian: "Do your best, let God do the rest, and pray for your teachers." For the sake of nostalgia, I'll still text those words to the kids now, so many years later.

These days as life has moved into a new season, the doorbell needs fixing and the landline has been disconnected. The music is always on but it has definitely changed. Bob and I can actually understand the words to the songs. The topics of conversation around the dining room table are less about building homecoming floats and finishing homework and more about cultivating community and acquiring real jobs. Who knew that our days would become less about book reports and more about writing books, less about practicing manners and more about caring for others overseas. Weddings, graduations, finding places to live, and starting careers—these are the main course now. The same chalkboard has been there in our home all along, witnessing our comings and goings like an old faithful friend. It seems no matter how much time passes, it continues to tell our next story, right where we left off with the last one.

I am discovering the beauty of the changing seasons, especially when everything that's possible in our lives now reflects everything we dreamed about and worked for then. I realize the learning curve is simply the arc of our lives. The lessons we're learning never really end because all of us are still growing, changing, and becoming better versions of ourselves. To the best of our ability, we still work life out together. Doing it this way made all the flaws, inadequacies, and strengths of our relationships stronger when things turned out far better or worse than we had planned. Life has continued to unfold for all of us as we pursue the things that matter the most—sharing love and admiration, respect and affirmation. Consistently aiming to declare the things we need here at home even when the world tries to tell us we should want something different.

I love watching the changes most in my kids. They have clearly moved from the season of preparing for what might come their way to living their plans and dreams. Their "someday" has arrived and their contribution in the world is in real time now. It turns out all those years of creating their own entertainment—forts out of cardboard boxes, imaginary towns in the neighborhood trees, playing air guitar in the garage, and dreaming up big ideas on warm summer nights—these were the warm-up bands to the soundtracks for the lives they're living now.

The stories we lived together when our kids were young are now retold by grown kids with bigger voices and deeper laughs. There is a depth of knowledge and familiarity that comes from being in the trenches together. There is a richness that comes in knowing each other's strengths and weaknesses. There is a power in understanding one another's journey, soft spots, and buttons. It all comes out when we're home.

The chalkboard in the kitchen has delivered countless messages to each of us over these years. We've each taken turns scratching out messages of hope and love and congratulations.

You've got this!
You are loved.
You did it!

If this chalkboard hanging on the wall of our kitchen could talk, it would tell stories of things we might want to forget, too. Like the time we attempted an awkward illustration about the birds and the bees once. The kids now affectionately call it our failed "chalk talk" as if we were football coaches explaining with lines and arrows a complicated play. But more importantly it would speak to a life we celebrated, people we welcomed, menus we served. Hopes and hugs all in white chalk against a dark background.

The chalkboard has been around for a couple decades now, and most of its important messages have been etched with broken pieces of broken chalk—a quiet reminder that God uses our brokenness to telegraph the most important messages to each other. These small pieces lay in a groove in the top of the frame, always available to any of us as we pass by to write what we're thinking about, hoping for, or even confused about. These words reach out to us with an invitation to add a few more to the narrative. Layer upon layer of our best and worst moments that turned into more than chalk dust in picture frame cracks. No one uses chalk without getting a little on them.

This is our way of highlighting what is important in the moment. We decided that the board was not a place to assign chores or to act as a reminder of who needs to be where and when. There are no hastily written notes to make anyone feel like they are in trouble. This is much more sacred, more meaningful, more uplifting. Anything that can be celebrated in life is etched there for everyone to see, an outer expression of our inner life. These are the personal markings of the passage of our time together. Like a pictograph on a caveman's wall, marking the things we declared important to our own family civilization.

The chalkboard became our family's way of declaring what we needed and believed to be true in our lives. It framed what was important to us, and it became tangible proof of a life fully lived. Chalky layers of love expressed over time are never completely erased. They don't need to be. The layers represent who we've become and who we are at our core. The things we deemed important are not perfectly drawn on perfect surfaces. Important things withstand the tests of time; they are markings that eventually become part of our family legacy.

It's important to take the time to engage in a life that is meaningful. It took us time to figure out what is truly important. That was time well spent. We get to decide what is important for ourselves and for our families. What we write on the chalkboard is one way we care for each other. It's our anchor hanging in the middle of the heart of our home. It's a declaration of our love for one another, giving importance to the things that matter. Regardless of whatever someone has written, the chalkboard always says home is a place where love is king, patience is practiced, joy is celebrated, and peace is served as the daily special.

We are gifted with this one life and we get to choose what we stand for. It's important to choose what that is rather than let it happen passively. We become who we are by practicing the things we know to be true. For my family it started by writing it down—in chalk. Every day these truths begin to marinate deep in our souls. Eventually, we are shaped by the choices we make, choices to create the family we want, shape the family we hope to have, influence who we become.

Our kids are grown now and I am proudly watching them influence those in their lives. They love gathering people around their tables, celebrating life together, and being there for one another. When Bob and I shift our focus in the summers to the place in Canada, we feel honored to welcome guests from all over the world. That place has a chalkboard, too, where we carefully write the words *Welcome Home* for each summer's set of guests. I see the effect these two words have on weary life-travelers. These words have the power to convey, no matter how far you have come, you are welcome right here, right now.

Whatever you declare as important to you, I hope it is done with intention, purpose, and reason. The world will constantly tell you what you should want, so we used the chalkboard to declare what we need. If you don't have a chalkboard, use your driveway. If you don't have a driveway, use the street. Better yet, leave your mark on the world. The residue you leave will be like layers of love leading you, your family, friends, and neighbors to a place called home for generations to come.

One last thought. I've often wondered what it will be like when we go from this last resting place we call home and move on to be with the One who made us for all of eternity. I'm not sure what heaven will look like. I imagine I'll start by looking for loved ones who have arrived before me. It makes me excited to think about the moment of entry, those first impressions. How cool would it be if hanging next to the gates of heaven, there is a huge gold-framed chalkboard covered with a millennium of chalky white dust from messages God has sent to each of us.

I bet God won't even try to brush off His hands as He winks and smiles at the giant letters on the board which simply read:

Welcome Home, love lives here.

In Their Own Words

We have three great kids and they all have amazing people they love. A few of our kids are married now, and our family got much better when they did. Our oldest daughter is Lindsey. We describe her as Mary Poppins—with grenades. She is supremely kind, fiercely loyal, and absolutely unafraid. She married a great guy named Jon. If God hadn't invented water, Jon would have. He's an engineer by day and MacGyver by night. I haven't seen anything he can't build or make. His heart is the size of Africa, and it's where you find him and Lindsey if they're not fixing up their home and baking pies to give away to neighbors and passersby.

Our oldest son, Richard, is creative, brave, and cares deeply for others. He's the guy who would fight you at a campfire for the one chair where all the smoke is going and then convince you he liked it better there. He's never taken a nap in his life. Instead, he would rather keep his sights on the next adventure. Richard is married to Ashley who is one of the smartest lawyers I know, but also one of the kindest ones, too. She's fiercely loyal, endlessly courageous, and has a humble spirit. If they aren't working on a house project, they are inviting people to their dinner table. Together they remind me about the quiet power that commitment and kindness have in our lives.

Adam is our youngest. He's fearless, to a fault. If there's a sport where you can't lose an arm, Adam's not interested. He's broken more than one bone in his body, but apparently keeps growing new ones, because he just keeps bouncing back up like nothing happened. I haven't seen an opportunity he's not up for engaging or a vehicle with an engine he's not interested in driving (really fast).

These are my people, the main characters in my life. Because of them, Bob and I are inspired to keep learning, growing, exploring, and loving to the best of our abilities.

I asked my grown kids if they had something they wanted to share with you. This is what they wrote.

Adam

My family has always had a different view of community. I grew up in a house that often hosted people from all over the world and from all different viewpoints. Many of these people were influencing culture by writing the books people are reading, making the movies people are watching, or just having an opinion that a lot of people did or didn't agree with. I suppose to some, our living room was like a scene out of *The League of Extraordinary Gentlemen*, but I never really saw it that way. A lot of times these people were tired, hurting, and just needed a place to breathe.

We have a tradition at the Lodge when we host retreats. On the last night, we gather in a circle to share what we've learned during the week. Writers share inspirational and contemporary outlooks on life. Foreign officials speak about peace and friendship with those they had despised only days before. Musicians and moviemakers share about their unique life experiences and meaningful conversations they had with each other. As they went around the circle recently, I realized that I was going to have to say something. Looking around the circle at who was there, I don't think I've ever felt less competent. The guy before me literally wrote the Bible. No really, he had just finished writing a completely new translation of the Bible. I was just learning how to write a haiku poem in school, and I ended up sitting next to the guy who did what Moses did. I was the youngest person in the room and felt like I had nothing to show from my short life except a killer baseball card collection.

I told them what it was like to be in my position as a kid watching big dreamers with big purpose live without fear of failure. I couldn't help but think that every person in the room had been in my shoes at some point. They were probably awkward and nerdy and looked a little like me, but at some point they each had said "yes" to a bold idea. These people influenced the world because they had taken risks and had not been afraid of big adventures with little certainty in outcomes.

Mom and Dad always talked about the idea of a "safety net" when we were growing up. "You're not flying without a net," they'd say to me when I tried something big and new and uncertain. When I think of a safety net, I think of tightrope walking—when you're trying to get your balance. If you've got a good net, you're not afraid to fall, because you know you'll be caught. I realize what changed everything for me is realizing that I'd be celebrated if I tried and safe if I fell. I grew up with the sense of a safety net always under me.

This is what it looks like for me now as an adult. If I have an idea, I assume it's worth trying. I learned from our friends in those circles that being young doesn't count against me; it works for me. I've also learned that royally screwing up doesn't count against me either. It makes me more ready for the next challenge.

These days, I spend a lot of time in a cubicle at my day job and spend my nights in classes for a graduate program. It would be easy to tell myself that I don't have free time anymore, but what people don't seem to talk about when you're growing up is how much life happens in the margins. I am constantly trying to fill out my margins— my lunch breaks, nights, and weekends. I'll give you an example. This year, I started skydiving. There is no better feeling than walking back into the office after lunch having just jumped out of a plane from 15,000 feet in a suit. These things are a blast and I'm my father's son, for sure; but what I'm learning now is that life can be a balance. While I work hard to build a stronger safety net for my kids I hope I'll have someday, I now know that I don't have to trade in my adventurous spirit to get there.

If I had kids, I would want to give them a combination of encouragement to go after their ideas and confirm for them that everyone who is older might look like they have it together. But actually, most of them have no clue what's going on either. The reality is that we are all more capable than we realize of creating a life of whimsy and adventure. We're not flying without a net because of the community we have and the opportunity to cultivate one (if we'll take the time). That's the mind-set I've grown up with: Take risks, say yes, fail big, and change the world. No matter who you are and where you are, you're never flying without a net.

Richard

"So what do you do for a living?"

Ugh, that's just the worst question. Nothing has ever made me feel more like a kid still pretending to be an astronaut. Trying to figure out what I want to be when I grow up has been the single toughest question for me to answer.

I grew up with an expectation of myself that I would do something great. That people would know my name because of what I did. My parents encouraged me to pursue my dreams and try anything, but I never felt like I had a clear target. Without a career in mind, I knew I wanted to be well liked, respected, and admired because I was as successful or influential as the people that I had admired growing up. That people would hear the name Richard Goff and think, *That guy's awesome.*

I met my wife Ashley when I was in the fourth grade. It wasn't until the end of high school that I had finally built up enough courage to ask her out. We dated for seven years, moved to different cities, graduated college, got her through law school, and found our way back to San Diego before I had built up enough courage to ask her the big question.

When I asked her to be Mrs. Goff, I was working part-time at a restaurant, looking for jobs on Craigslist, and I was living on a dumpy little sailboat that was only floating because of a delicate combination of duct tape and intense prayer. When I asked Ashley to marry me, I was anything but sure of what I was going to be. I had no money, no direction, and little confidence in my ability to "adult."

One evening, I took Ashley out on my little boat and putted out into the bay. When we were out past the docks, but still close enough to swim for it, I raised the yellowed, tired-looking sail where a friend who worked at a sail shop had sown giant letters that spelled out "will you marry me?" It was like all the most romantic parts of *Titanic*, including the sinking part. Despite my uncertainty and lack of direction, she said "yes." It didn't hinge on how many people knew my name because she knew who I was.

I hadn't truly realized the value of my name until Ashley agreed to make it her own.

We've been married now for a couple years and I'm less concerned about what I do, or who knows me because I am truly known by her, by my family, my friends, and hopefully the future generations that I'll never get to meet. Career stuff all works out. It finds its footing as we take more steps. I now work for an awesome company that makes ugly Christmas sweaters (of course), but the true mark of my success has been the admiration of those who love me. My career and who I am are not the same. Having my name recognized is not how I measure my worth, and how much I make in a year doesn't represent my value. Ashley, my parents, and my entire family have helped me learn that my career isn't what I do for a living—*they* are what I do for a living.

Lindsey

When Jon and I fell in love he asked me, "So, how does a guy get engaged to Lindsey Goff?" I was impressed by his question. In response, I told him that when I was growing up, I woke up each day to the sound of my parents talking in their chairs in the living room. My dad always sat in the one on the right, mom in the left, framing the fireplace with cups of coffee in their hands. They couldn't have spent more than five minutes in those chairs before my brothers and I broke the peace with our joyful chaos. But for those five minutes, it was just the two of them talking. I don't even know what they talked about—maybe they talked about us, or a house project, or whether or not to get a dog. Regardless, as a little girl the takeaway for me was clear: Marriage is about sitting in your chairs, together, every morning.

When Jon asked me that question—how does a guy get engaged to Lindsey Goff?—I already knew that I didn't want a ring. Like my mom, I've never been a big jewelry person. I'd watched countless friends get engaged and upon sharing the news, I would watch people excitedly reach for my friends' left hand, looking for the ring. That was, of course, sweet—and to this day I have nothing against rings. I always had an inkling of a thought, though, as I contemplated marriage, that it would be really neat to have the symbol of engagement also be a real symbol of marriage. Instead of people saying, "Let me see your ring!" I pictured them instead saying, "Let me see your fiancé!"

I grew up in a family where sentimentality reigns. I grew up in a home where practicality was frequently ignored in the name of whimsy, meaning, and legacy. Getting engaged was no different. I knew if I was going to get engaged to Jon, I didn't want a ring. Instead, as a symbol of our marriage to come, I wanted us to get two chairs.

One of our cherished family holidays is New Year's Day when we gather together with our neighborhood to have a parade. That year at our parade, Jon surprised me with two darling, charming, and perfect navy blue wingback chairs. I later found out that Jon had found the two chairs on Craigslist and lovingly spent hundreds of hours reupholstering them in my favorite color. They were waiting at the top of the hill, hidden behind two huge clusters of balloons in his hands.

To this day, our little blue chairs sit in the living room of our home. We sit in them often. Most days, it's to chat or eat dinner, but sometimes, when we have a hard day or get bad news, we go immediately to our blue chairs. The informal tradition I learned from my own family now carries on in ours, and it has become a beautiful part of our marriage and the culture we're creating.

———————

Richard, Adam, Jon, and Bob are the kind of men I'd hope to surround myself with. They're strong, humble, and honest. Lindsey and Ashley are the kind of women I'd hope to surround myself with, too. They are also strong, humble, and honest. Each of these remarkable people knows who they are and while incredibly intuitive, they don't presume to know who everyone else is. They just love people, as they are; where they are. In these ways and more, they remind me of the way Jesus lived His life. Fully engaged, courageous, and immensely loving. These are my people. The ones who help me find what I need the most. They are my world and my epicenter and why love doesn't live somewhere else; it lives right here.

Acknowledgments

Writing can feel a lot like single-handed sailing across a big ocean in a small boat. It's at times a lonely, scary, and crazy journey. What I discovered in writing these words is also true in our lives. None of us are ever alone. Instead, our friends are the wind at our back. Flipping through the pages of this book I see the evidence of so many friends who have quietly, diligently, and sacrificially traveled with me on this voyage. They've never looked for applause. Just like the wind never asks to be thanked for how far it took the boat, they've never asked to be acknowledged for all they have done. This is my attempt.

At the end of a great adventure it's the people who get you there. The one's who rolled up their sleeves, hoisted the sails or lifted the anchor when I felt stuck. Like you, they care about love and connection and they're willing to learn, grow, and do what it takes to help their friends. They are kind and funny, humble and helpful, and they constantly reminded me that I was not alone on this journey. The crew has been large and the distance traveled was great. I'm grateful for the many people who helped get me to shore.

In the beginning there was Bob. I am convinced he's the guy God sent to show me how much He loved me no matter what. He has always believed in me more than I believe in myself. Bob's faith, love, and constant encouragement are like helium to my soul when I start to sink under the pressures I put on myself. Bob knows he isn't perfect, but he is as good, kind, and funny as he is smart, capable, and wise. Most of all, he loves God in a way that inspires me to want to know Him more, too. There isn't anyone I'd rather be tied to while scaling a cliff than him. All I need to hear him say is, "I've got you" and I'm good.

Lindsey, Jon, Richard, Ashley, and Adam are our favorite part of every single day. Their own lives are my favorite stories. They've taught me more about believing, dreaming, and finding the best way over and around the hot lava in my life when it unexpectedly shows up. Their extravagant, over-the-top, amazing brand of love is the only proof I need that God is good.

On more than one occasion wise counselors have helped me clear away my own charred logs and debris. Trustworthy people like Stephanie, Miles, Jim, Laurie, Bill, and my friends at Onsite. They gave me the tools like a pick, an axe, and a headlamp to find my own buried treasures.

Then there is Bryan Norman, who is so good at being my friend he's never felt like my literary agent. We've covered a lot of ground since the day we stood on a dock in the Canadian Rockies and talked about the possibility of bringing this book to life. His depth of knowledge is impressive, but what I've come to appreciate even more is his ability to stay on course when the storms (and tears) came while I wrote.

When I met my friends at B&H Publishing: Jennifer Lyell, Devin Maddox, and Dave Schroeder, they didn't need to impress me, they had me at "hello." Everyone there who was a part of bringing this book to life gave me the courage I needed to keep my eyes on my own paper.

Long before we knew this book would be published, I received a check as a preorder for the first copy. That check has sat in a frame on my desk for the past three years. It's been awhile, but I am happy to finally say to Emily and Bryson, "Your copy of the book is in the mail."

I'm not sure if guardian angels are assigned to watch over books as they're written, but if there is, these ones have worked overtime. To Tara, Hilary, Kari, Anne Marie, Jan, Beth, Whitney, Vanessa, Jill, Kate, Jess, Angela, Sarah, Cayt, and the Loves Does Team, a thousand times thank you for your notes, prayers, video messages and word of encouragement. I'm also grateful to Don, Betsy, Shauna, Lysa, Shelley, Ryan, Mike, Bianca, Jay, Katherine, Jeremy, and Jennie for being the first to read what I wrote and giving me the guts to send it to the publisher when it was finished.

Many thanks to the countless people we've met through Young Life's Malibu Camp next door to us in Canada. The property staff, assignment teams, summer staff, work crew, and people like Terri, Harold, Paul, and Dorothee are heroes to us. You've been the kind of neighbors who have taught me that faith is more than a little blue scarf and Neapolitan ice cream. It's expressed in a thousand acts of love strung together by a belief in something bigger than any of us.

It is impossible to know the exact number of friends we've hosted in our home over the years. Thank you to each of you for what you've taught me about letting love set the table. You've been the teachers; I've been the student.

When I hung a help wanted sign in my front window I knew one of the things I needed was a good sitter for my kids. We found that help in a fun and energetic college girl named Hollyn. When she grew up, got married, and started raising kids of her own she asked me, "How do you do it? Marriage, kids, life?" I am not sure I was able to give her an answer back then, but my hope when I wrote this book was to add what I've learned to what she already knows.

God gives each of us a few people who we get the privilege of doing life with for decades. These are the one's who teach us love's ways through their availability and kindness.

Many thanks to Mike and Melissa McDonald, Rob and Leslie Hanna, Chuck and Laurie Driscoll, Michael and Debbie Smith, Steve and Janet Murray, Rick and Marti Parker, and Doug and Debbie Ament.

And finally, to you who have held this book in your hand, or listened to it, thank you for stepping into the boat. Thank you for spending this time with me. You are not alone on this journey either. May the sun rise up to meet you every day, may God's wind remain at your back and may you always know where love lives.

Writers say you never really finish a book you just stop writing. Here's where I stop writing.

The End

Connect with Maria

I hope you've enjoyed reading this book as much as I've enjoyed writing it. Perhaps there are questions you have about what your next steps forward will be. I know I would learn so much from you and your life experiences.

Bob wrote a book called *Love Does* and he put his phone number on the last page. I thought he was nuts when he did. Since then, he's answered thousands of phone calls from people from every generation, denomination, and geographical location. People call him from hospitals, Bible studies, schools, and prisons. Most of the people who call want to know if he'll actually answer his phone. The crazy part is—he does. I'm an introvert who would love to hear from you. So, if you want to reach me, here's Bob's cell phone number (619) 985-4747. My favorite place to be is next to him, so perhaps he can pass the phone to me.

WEBSITE: LoveLivesHereBook.com

INSTAGRAM: @sweetmariagoff

TWITTER: @sweetmariagoff

FACEBOOK: /SweetMariaGoff